DREAM IT
and
BUILD IT

How to

CRUSH YOUR REAL ESTATE INVESTING GOALS

JOSIAH SMELSER

Dream It and Build It

© 2020 by Josiah Smelser

ISBN (Print): 978-1-54399-366-0
ISBN (eBook): 978-1-54399-367-7

Sarah - thank you for loving me through thick and thin and supporting me as I chase my dreams.

Eden, Hannah, and Isaac - you can do it. I love you and am in your corner always. I love you four more than you know

Dream It and Build It

How to Crush Your Real Estate Investing Goals

By

Josiah Smelser

Each of us are on a journey, even though our journeys are different. My goal was to achieve financial freedom through real estate investing, and if you picked up this book, your interest is likely the same. Financial freedom can come in all shapes and sizes depending on your life goals, such as: freedom to do work you love, freedom to quit your nine to five, having enough money to retire when you would like, having enough money to travel, having enough money to give freely, etc. We were all created differently, and therefore will use our talents in different ways to reach our different goals.

I owned no real estate and was debt free when I started with little investment capital. I partnered 50/50 with my best friend who had some money saved and wanted someone with knowledge and hustle to help him build a real estate investment portfolio. My partner and I created an audacious goal—we wanted to buy ten properties worth a total of $2 million at 75% loan-to-value in 12 months using the BRRRR strategy (buy, rehab, rent, refinance, and repeat). We took massive action and acquired 15 properties worth roughly $3 million in only 12 months using a value add investing strategy. Here is the crazy part—we have a lender that will refinance this portfolio at 80%

loan-to-value, which allows us to get *all our investment capital back.* My partner contributed our initial investment capital and we now have $900k in equity in our cash flowing rental properties. At 80% loan-to-value, we have none of our own capital locked in and 20% equity, or $600k equity in a $3 million dollar cash flowing real estate portfolio. How did we do it? It all comes down to mind-set, a refusal to quit, and an intentional way of approaching investing.

This book was written over the past 12 months as my partner and I built our $3 million dollar real estate portfolio. Each entry is written as a reflection on what I observed in both my investing business as well as fellow investors' businesses. There are formulas and numbers sprinkled throughout, but this book is not meant to be a formulaic textbook. Ninety-five percent of your real estate investing results will come from your mindset, and this book was written for that very purpose: to get your mind right. My goal is to arm you for success and support you on this journey.

You need 3 things to successfully build a real estate portfolio, and you only have to possess one of the three to be bring value. You can partner to fill in the gaps with the two you don't possess:

1. Hustle
2. Money
3. Knowledge

But my specific story is irrelevant to you, because your journey will be different than mine, and comparing what you have to others is a losing proposition. Whether you have no real estate or have billions in real estate, this book is for you. This book is meant to help you find peace in the chaos; to feel settled in as the problems come streaming in, because they will. Real estate is a problem-solving game, and a beautiful one at that. The joy is in the journey, and by adopting a peaceful mind-set, you can not only accomplish your financial goals and achieve financial freedom, but you can do it in an incredibly fun and comfortable way.

I hope these words inspire you to keep trying. Don't quit. Don't lose heart. Your freedom is right on the other side of these obstacles, and as Ryan Holiday so poignantly wrote, "the obstacle is the way. Do it, and do it your way, and find peace in your quest." Let's go!

Financial Freedom through Real Estate Investing

"Having goals is great—but it's not enough! You need
action, too! You will need to get off your butt and change
the world yourself, because no one else will do it for you."

—Brandon Turner

There are several ways to achieve financial freedom through real estate investing. All have benefits as well as drawbacks, but here are my favorite six ways:

1. Own buy and hold rental real estate. Keep it rented and let the tenants pay off the property while it appreciates in value and you pocket the surplus cash flow. Use the BRRRR (buy, rehab, rent, refinance, repeat) strategy to build a cash-cow of a portfolio.
2. Flip real estate properties: buy distressed, fix up, and sell for a profit.
3. Wholesale: take control of a property through a contract to purchase and find another party who is willing to buy it from you (the middle man) at a premium.
4. Property management: manage rental real estate for an owner and receive a fee.
5. Brokerage: Receive a commission for the purchase, sale, or leasing of real estate.
6. Lending: Lend money to others for their real estate deals.

The beautiful thing about all of the above options is that each one can be done by building a system and taking yourself out of the equation. Financial freedom (to me) means the ability to pay your bills with the passive income your business is producing. There are many meanings to passive, but when I say passive in this context, I mean passive in the aspect that the money can be earned without your specific involvement. This requires you to build a system and work on your business and not in your business (*EMyth Revisited*).

The Math to Reach Financial Independence

"By setting the goal to achieve financial independence using real estate investing, you're creating space for your important dreams."

—Chad Carson from *Retire Early With Real Estate*

I am greatly interested in the concept of F.I. (financial independence), preferably as soon as reasonably possible. There are many methods of achieving this goal, and one of these is through using real estate. Let me give you an example of a simple real estate route to accomplishing F.I. Let's say you want to have $2,000,000 in an index fund and plan to live off of 4% per year while the fund compounds at roughly 8% per year. Adjusted for 2% yearly inflation, you could take your 4% per year in perpetuity while your money continues to grow 2% per year adjusted for inflation. This would mean you could live on $80k per year (before tax). If $80k before tax covers your yearly living expenses with money left over, you are financially independent.

Here is a simple way to do this through real estate in 10–12 years.

Years 1–2 buy 15 value add properties using hard money (start with 5 the first year and then 10 the second), then after getting them renovated, refi them over to fixed long-term financing. You can do 10 through Fannie Mae, and go through the commercial side of the banks for the other five. It's up to you how you finance them. I recommend getting them set up on fixed financing so you mitigate the risk of rates rising and you have having to renew your loan at a higher rate. You could start with 1 house at a time and shoot for five deals year 1, then move up to 2 or 3 houses at a time in year 2 once you have mastered the process. If it takes you 3 years instead of 2, no big deal. Make sure once your value add process is complete, you have 25% or more equity (or as close to it as you can get) in your properties and you can recover your initial investment so you can repeat the process. Let's say you purchase your average property for $80k, fix up + holding + closing costs = $20k, so you are all in for $100k. The property appraises for $150k upon your refi, so you now have 33% equity with a debt of $100k on average. Put these properties on a 15 year note, and aggressively pay them down. In 10 years, nearly 58% of the debt will be paid off, or roughly $41k of debt will remain on each property. If you purchase in solid areas (which you should and you will), you will get a healthy appreciation rate which we will estimate at 3.5% for this example (it is very possible for you to get better than 3.5% annually in the right areas). To figure out what your properties will be worth in 10 years, plug the following calculation into Excel: $150k x 1.035 ^ 10 = $212k value approximately. Sell all your properties after 10 years, so you have approximately $212k–$41k = $171k profit per property. $171k x 15 = $2.6 million dollars. Let's say we lose 10% in the sales process from closing costs and repairs, so we net approximately $2.3 million. We then pay long-term capital gains of 15% (check the current rate) and net roughly $2 million. Let's say you choose not to 1031 the profits into other properties, but choose to simplify your life with zero debt and mailbox money. Easy enough.

Take your $2 million and invest it a low cost diversified index fund at Vanguard. I recommend VTSMX, the Vanguard Total Stock Market Index fund—very diversified and very low cost. Set the fund up to send you approximate 4% of the fund value (between dividend payments and sales of shares) and bam—you have $80k in mailbox money and no debt! The logic behind the 4% rule holds that on average, if you live off of only 4% of your funds (between dividends and share sales), your nest egg $2 million should grow indefinitely. Another words, on average, VTSMX should return more than 4% (dividends included) and net of the 4% you are withdrawing, still grow. Monte Carlo simulations have been run on this 4% rule theory, and the study shows that the 4% is legit based on past stock market growth and decline cycles. Get on Google and read up on it.

Real estate is a very powerful thing if used the right way.

Cash on Cash Return

"It all comes down to interest rates. As an investor, all you're doing is putting up a lump sum payment for a future cash flow."

—Ray Dalio

Cash on cash return is one of most popular and most commonly used metrics in real estate investing. The formula for cash on cash return is:

Cash on Cash Return: Net Profit/Cash Invested

For instance, if I purchase a $100k property and put $20k down, $20k would be my cash invested. If after all expenses and debt service I have net profit of $5,000 for the year, then my cash on cash return would be calculated as follows: $5,000/$20,000 = 25% cash on cash return.

The beauty of real estate investment is the use of leverage or debt to control a valuable asset with very little of your own money relative to the total value of the property. In our example we controlled a $100k property with only $20,000 out of our pocket, so we carried $80k in debt and $20k in equity. Another way to think of this example would be with only $1 invested, we were able to control $5 worth of real estate.

On my deals, I generally look for a value add play. Buy something distressed, get it fixed up, get it rented out, then do a cash out refinance to recover my initial cash investment. Sometimes I manage to get all my initial cash investment back with extra cash, which is great. Sometimes, I just get my initial cash back, in which case my cash on cash return would be infinite. And in other cases, I get *most* of my initial cash back and can run a cash on cash calculation. Let's look at an example where I get most of my cash back.

Purchase distressed property $60k
Repair costs/finance and holding costs/closing costs $20k
Total investment $80k
After repair value (ARV) via appraisal $100k
Cash out refinance max loan to value per bank 75% loan to value
Property is rented and net income after debt payment is $1k for the year

To run these numbers, I first need to see how much money I will get from the bank once my property is refinanced. This calculation is after repair value via appraisal of $100k x 75% loan to value = $75,000 new debt

I spent a total of $80,000 (purchase + renovation and all other costs), so I will only get $75,000 refinanced into the new debt. $80k (initial investment)—$75k (new debt from refinance) = $5k net cash invested

Net debt $75k
Asset value $100k
Total cash investment after refi $5k
Total net profit after debt service $1k
Cash on cash return net profit/cash investment = $1k/$5k = 20% cash on cash return

It's a beautiful thing, right? For only $5,000 of my own money invested, I was able to buy a cash flow rental property worth $100k with $25k in equity! On top of that, not including principle paydown or depreciation benefits, I am receiving a take-home profit after debt service of $1k on my $5k investment. If I put this property on a 30 year note, I will now let the tenant pay this property off for me while

I take my 20% return and reinvest it in more projects. Let's say this property appreciates at 3.5% annually for the next 30 years because we bought in a solid area. A quick calculation: $100k x 1.035^30 = $280k

So in 30 years, when this baby is paid off, my property would be worth around $280k! Not a bad return on simply putting $5k in, right? A whopping 56x our investment, and this doesn't even take into consideration our $1k profit every year! This is why I love real estate!

Flipping Houses

"The Flip Formula: Maximum Purchase Price (MPP)
= Sales Price, Fixed Costs, Profit, and Rehab Costs."

—J Scott, *The Book on Flipping Houses*

Flipping houses is a job—make no mistake. Flipping can be a very lucrative job if done correctly, or a very poor one if one doesn't know what they are doing. Either way—it is a job. When the house is sold, the cash-generating asset is gone. Investing in buy and hold real estate builds long-term wealth.

Of the successful house flippers I have interviewed on the podcast, here is what I have found as a common factor that make them successful. They have a created a well-oiled machine—a system.

Successful house flipping system:

1. Streamlined acquisition and disposition process
2. Trustworthy and competent contractors doing the work in a cost-efficient and timely manner
3. Detailed product list (down to the sku # and color) for what is generally used in every flip
4. Working/fruitful relationships with lenders (hard money, private money, banks, etc.)
5. Proper cash reserves

If any of the above five factors are missing, the flip can quickly go from great to a money loser. And no flipper hits homeruns on every swing. Most flippers I have interviewed (that flip homes in the Southeast) average $20k–$30k a flip, with some much higher and breaking even or even losing money on occasion. Cash is king, so having a proper amount on cash in reserves is essential to staying in this game.

Once the home is sold, the flipper (hopefully) now has a check in their hand for all the hard work performed and now typically has to pay short-term capital gains tax (holding an asset for less than one year before sale). Let's say you just made $20,000 for a 3 month flip start to finish (acquisition to sale). Let's assume a short-term capital gains tax rate of 25% (check the current as this is always subject to change). You will owe 25% of $20k or $5k to Uncle Sam in taxes, so you really only netted $15k for all that work. Now $15k isn't bad, but it isn't as sweet as $20k. The tax implications are certainly one major point to consider.

The takeaway—build your system. Start with the end in mind— the end in this situation being the goal of flipping homes while not requiring your presence. To do this, the system must run without you. You will check in to make sure everything is on track with the goal of even hiring this task out. Start small, learn as you do more and more flips, build your team, then scale.

Smart Money

"Games are won by players who focus on the playing field—not by those whose eyes are glued to the scoreboard. If you instead focus on the prospective price change of a contemplated purchase, you are speculating. There is nothing improper about that. I know, however, that I am unable to speculate successfully, and I am skeptical of those who claim sustained success at doing so."

—Warren Buffett

In my early 30s, I made a stock investment with $65,000 that turned into $250,000 in about 6 months. I was giddy, watching the stock ticker relentlessly as the pundits predicted the stock to continue its meteoric rise. It was predicted to turn my shares into over a million dollars in less than a few more months.

Then, as sure as it had gone up, it came crashing down. $200k. $175k. $150k. I was frozen.

The experts said, "Ride it out. Don't sell. It is only a correction."

The stock continued its plummet back to $65k. I finally pulled the trigger and sold it. For that insane ride, I made absolutely nothing.

"Why didn't you sell sooner?" you may wonder.

If I had known the stock was going to go straight down, selling would have been obvious.

Warren Buffett says you can't watch the scoreboard, and I think that is why Buffett has been so successful in stock investing while the average person flounders. It is hard not to get emotional about your money while watching it fluctuate by the second, and that is why there is so much emotional buying and selling in the stock market. The

Wall Street moguls label this the "dumb money." (Seeing some of their historic returns, I am not so sure they aren't dumb money as well.)

We can choose to be the "smart money" instead—by investing in an asset class that we can steadily ride to success, one that doesn't constantly flash a price in our face and can therefore save us from ourselves. That is why I love real estate. There is no ticker flashing, telling you what someone is willing to pay for your property every second of the day. Instead, there are the facts that make the investment more or less predictable—cash flow, debt pay down, appreciation, and tax advantages.

I don't know about you, but I have consistently been able to pull off higher rates of return on my real estate investments than on my investments in the stock market. And that feels like smart money to me.

The takeaways:

- Keep your eyes on the playing field and off of the scoreboard.
- Hang on for the long haul.
- Never make emotional decisions.
- Don't speculate; keep to the hard facts.
- Real estate investment makes these rules easy to keep.

Becoming Unemployable

*"A penguin cannot become a giraffe, so just
be the best penguin you can be."*

—Gary Vaynerchuk

Today I am thinking about all the cubicles I sat in before taking the plunge to do real estate full time and becoming my own boss. Man was it worth it.

I had a job offer recently where they basically offered me a little more money than my current self-employed income to sacrifice all my time and flexibility, and it was at that point that I realized that I have become unemployable. I'm not unemployable from the perspective that I can't do good work for someone else on a W2 salary income, but unemployable from the perspective that I have discovered how to make a great living running my own business doing work I love with total flexibility.

What is there to gain by starting your own business and becoming unemployable?

I do exactly the work I love. I control my schedule. I control what I wear to work. I control whether or not I want to grow a beard. I control when I work and when I don't work. I control firing a nuisance of a client. I control when I take my vacations, how long I vacation, and where I work from. I control when I answer phone calls and when I send to voicemail. I control when to explore a new business idea. I control when I exercise, when I take a long lunch, or when I stop work for the day and go to a movie. I control when I go to bed. I control who I am becoming. I control my day.

There are millions of people who are living stuck lives. Stuck dressing like they don't want to, sitting in a cubicle where they don't want to, having awkward lunches with people they don't want to be with, doing work they don't want to do, and becoming people they don't want to become. There is another way. The other way will be a grind and you will fail a lot and likely be poor for a while, but man, it is so worth it. And you will wake up one day and realize that you have come unemployable.

Just Try

*"It is common sense to take a method and try it. If it fails,
admit it frankly and try another. But above all, try something."*

—Franklin D. Roosevelt

My 4 year-old daughter begged to sign up for soccer this year. She loves soccer and impressed us when she took off dribbling a soccer ball in the backyard at only 2 years old. Naturally, because she wanted to play soccer and I am a fan of trying things I have never done before in order to stretch and grow, I signed up to coach the 3- and 4-year-old co-ed soccer team.

During our first practice, when a player would run at my daughter, she would shy away from contact, come and hang on my leg, and in tears, exclaim, "I don't want to play anymore. I just want to sit out."

I tried everything to encourage her to give it a shot, but with tears rolling down her cheeks, she refused. Game day rolled around, and we had the same result. She started off in the game, but begged to come out of the game the second people started running towards her, in tears.

On the way home, I explained to her that she needed to finish what she had begged to start.

"I am not asking you to be good at soccer, I am not even asking you to kick the ball, but I simply want you to run around and give it your best shot. You asked to play soccer a number of times, so I signed up to coach you. You need to try. That is all I am asking. I just want you to stay on the field and try."

"But I am scared, Dad."

"What is scaring you?" I asked.

"I am scared that I won't know what to do."

"Don't worry about knowing what to do. Just stay out there, run around, and have fun. You can kick the ball if it comes your way, but if not, that's okay, too. You can do it. I've seen you dribble the ball across the backyard like a professional soccer player."

"Okay," she said.

Next game she started on the field, same as the last. The score was 0–0, and a boy twice her size on the other team dribbled the ball straight at her. This time she ran towards the boy, took the ball away from him, and sprinted through the crowd of boys and girls with the ball right at her feet. As she dribbled through the crowd of kids until she was all alone and then kicked the ball straight into the goal, tears welled up in my eyes. I had sunglasses on, and it is a good thing I did, because tears were rolling down my cheeks.

I ran and picked her up and carried her over my shoulder as she screamed, "Dad! I scored!"

"I'm so proud of you! I said. I'm proud of you scoring a goal, but I am even more proud of you for trying!"

Our team won that game 5–3, and my daughter scored 4 of our 5 goals.

This is us, right? We want so badly to play the game of real estate, but when we enter the game, we freeze up, cry for help, and take ourselves back out of the game. I don't know what to do. I'm scared. I need help. I don't have enough experience. I can't do this on my own. I might embarrass myself. I might fail. There are people or things in my way. I don't know how to reach the goal from here.

I am here to tell you this—you have what it takes to play the game, and to win the game; however, you must conquer your fear of failure and get in the game. You will experience hardships during the game, but you will also have moments where you take the ball down the field through the obstacles and put it squarely in the back of the net. You can do it. Just try.

Margin of Safety

"Price is what you pay. Value is what you get."

—Warren Buffet

The sage of stock investing gave us a golden nugget for real estate investing as well. There is no concept more important in becoming a successful real estate investor than the margin of safety concept. The more margin you have (or equity you have) in a deal, the less risky (or safer), the investment. Too much equity and leveraged returns diminish. Too little equity and the slightest hiccup takes your cash flow negative.

Buffet also says, "Rule number one—never lose money. Rule number two—never forget rule number one."

My goal in each of my holdings is to buy something with value add potential. Maybe it needs cosmetic rehab to realize top dollar in the market, maybe the asset is not stabilized and needs a few units brought online and leased out to stabilize cash flow, or maybe the property needs a new management team in place. When I recognize value add potential in a deal, that gets me interested. I then run my numbers and do my homework, and if I can achieve my desired cash on cash return and walk into equity (margin of safety), I pull the trigger. How much equity or margin of safety you require is up to you. I shoot for a minimum of 20% and prefer 25% or more if possible. Attaining a margin of safety in your investment deals is what separates the investors who experience great success from those who flounder.

Compound Interest Can Make You Very Wealthy over Time

"The power of compound interest is the most powerful force in the universe."

—Albert Einstein

I put together an IRR calculation on a single-family deal we just did. Here is how the numbers shook out once the deal was done. We purchased the property in foreclosure for a great price and then fixed up the property with new flooring, new paint, new appliances, new granite, and a new subway tile backsplash. We were all in for $175,000 (purchase price+ holding costs/refi costs + renovations). We rented the property out to well qualified tenants and then proceeded with a cash-out refi. On the cash-out refi, the property appraised for $230,000. We received 75% of the $230k appraised value, so we got $172,500. As our cost in this investment was a total of $175,000 and we refinanced $172,500 of this initial amount, we ended up only investing $2,500 in this completely renovated property that is leased to quality tenants and has a cash flow (net of all expenses and debt service) of $250 per month. We now have a $172,500 debt on a 25-year note on a property currently worth $230,000. For our creativity and sweat equity, we walked into nearly $55k in new equity (not including our $2,500) on this property based on its current value. I put together an IRR calculation for us, and I think Warren Buffett would be proud. We initially invested $2,500, and in 25 years at 3% annual appreciation, we would sell this property and receive net $482k. Excluding rental profit, that is 192x our initial $2,500 investment and an internal rate of return (IRR) of 102.8%! You can find deals like this too, just get out there, deal hunt, and make some offers. Persistence is the name of the game.

Our deal numbers:

Property Purchase Price	$ 150,000
Renovations/Holding & Refi Costs	$ 25,000
After Repair Value	$ 230,000
Equity Investment	$ 2,500
Hold Period (Years)	25
Annual Appreciation Rate	3.0%
Rent Appreciation Rate	2.5%
Future Value	$ 481,569
Profit Per Month	$ 209
IRR	**102.8%**

Become a Pro

"The Spartan king Agesilaus was still fighting in armor when he was eighty-two. Picasso was painting past ninety, and Henry Miller was chasing women (I'm sure Picasso was too) at eighty-nine. Once we turn pro, we're like sharks who have tasted blood, or renunciants who have glimpsed the face of God. For us, there is no finish line. No bell ends the bout. Life is the pursuit. Life is the hunt. When our hearts burst... then we'll go out, and no sooner."

—Steven Pressfield, *Turning Pro*

I read a book yesterday that blew my mind. The book is *Turning Pro*, by Steven Pressfield. Get the book right now if you don't already have it. Few things are worth well over 100 times what you pay for them, but this book is one of them.

Pressfield makes the case for turning pro instead of remaining an amateur operating as your shadow self. Pressfield calls us out on having dreams but living a timid shadow life, only a mere fraction of what we could be if we shook off "the Resistance" of addition, self-loathing, self-degradation, and caring what others think of our dreams. To turn pro is to embrace your craft for the sake of it being your calling, your talent, your bright spot to add to the world. You have gold inside, but many times only polish and mine the coal. Bring the gold out—mask off—into the sunlight. Chase your dreams without a care for what everyone else will think while you develop yourself into the pro that sleeps inside. You have greatness, and many times, we are actually terrified to let it show. Let's make a deal—from now until our last breath we live as pros, not amateurs. We don't waste life anymore.

Getting Rid of Negative Energy in Your Life

"I had to do a clearing in my life of some people whose energy, I realized, was not supportive of who I wanted to be in the world. And I recognized there were people who were not going to take responsibility for their energy, so I now have to take responsibility for the energy that I allow to be brought into my space. Life changing for me. And what I know is, you cannot continue to move forward in your life to the level, and level, and level that you need to be if you're surrounded by energy that brings you down, that sucks the life force from you, so not only are you responsible for the energy you bring, what I learned, you are also responsible for the energy you surround yourself with. Huge, huge, huge, huge. And everybody who is watching me right now, I know that you know this is true. There are some energy suckers in your life, just literally taking the life force out of you, and you will never be able to do and be who you are supposed to be in the world as long as you continue to buy into the energy suckers."

—Oprah Winfrey

This wisdom from Oprah is so powerful. There are people around us that bring negativity into our lives. It comes in many different forms and fashions—a discouraging word, simply not supporting you as you chase your dreams, ignoring your victories when you need their love, shooting down your ideas, or generally keeping you at arms-length and staying connected to you, but not being in your corner. These people can't be close to you and you become the person you need to be. Cut that negative energy out of your life and never look back. Life is too short to not realize your potential because someone else isn't in your corner. Let it motivate you that they won't get behind you, and never look back.

You Will Die One Day

*"Every man's life ends the same way. It is only
the details of how he lived and how he died
that distinguish one man from another."*

—Ernest Hemingway

We are all going to die. You have a certain number of days left, and then your time will be up, same as the generations before you, as well as the generations after. If you could sit in attendance at your funeral and observe unbeknownst to all, what would people say about your life? What do you want them to say?

Here is what I want to hear at my funeral:

- He passionately loved God, his family, and his friends.
- He tried to help as many people as he could.
- He wasn't afraid to step out and pursue his dreams.
- He didn't give up.

Take time to write down several things you want people to say about you when your days are over. Once you have written them down, observe exactly what it is you truly value. In light of this observation, align your business and real estate goals to support what is most important to you, and never compromise.

Cash Flow is Key

"Remember, this business is more than today's numbers. Real estate trades on future assumptions of income growth or contraction. Your ability to anticipate future cash flow should dramatically influence the financial structuring you do today."

—Ben Leeds

The driver of value in investment real estate is typically the cash flow it produces. Unless you have a speculation play on a piece of land or something of that nature that is yet to produce cash flow, your lifeblood is the property's cash flow (or dividend) production.

This cash flow is a function of the future assumptions of income growth or contraction associated with your micro-market (location), your tenant base, and your property type. Pay close attention to the big picture of where your overall market is trending, and then drill down to your micro-market and do the same. There are good and bad micro-markets located in most every market. Your hope is to locate a good micro-market in a stable larger market and make your investments within a margin of safety in those areas. Cusp areas on the fringe of good micro-markets in stable larger markets are a great place to invest and experience outsized returns.

Long-Term Real Estate Owners Grow Wealthy

"Don't wait to buy real estate. Buy real estate and wait."

—Will Rogers

Real estate is a get rich slow scheme, which I believe is the very best way to build and maintain wealth over time. There are many stories of people winning the lottery or coming into vast amounts of money overnight, but almost each and every case ends up back where they started— frustrated, and with their new found wealth a memory of the past. The reason for this is that they did not develop the skill set to manage wealth in the process of acquiring the wealth. This is extremely dangerous. One would be much better off to develop the skill set to manage wealth and never acquire the wealth itself, rather than acquiring the wealth with no skill set to manage it.

As you slowly build wealth, you will build the skill set to manage that wealth. If you're a poor manager and do not develop the skills needed to manage your real estate, you will not succeed. It is imperative that you manage your properties with an eye for optimization and eliminating waste. View your properties as tiny, living, breathing businesses in need of a CEO and customers, and in need of your attention to thrive. If maintained and run well by their CEO, these little businesses will make you money while you sleep.

Don't wait to buy real estate. Don't talk about being an investor and never pull the trigger. Holding real estate long term will cover up a number of missteps up front, as long as they weren't colossal missteps. The reason holding long term works is the beauty of property appreciation through compound interest, principal paydown, and rising rental rates.

Find a Niche and Focus on It

*"Don't try to reinvent the wheel. Just focus on
making it better than everyone else."*

—John Muir

As a real estate investor, there is no need to reinvent the wheel. Find a niche that resonates with you and learn what those who are successful in this niche have done to achieve their success. If you developed competence in an area of real estate before becoming an investor, start in your area of competence and build out from there.

For example, I learned real estate by starting as a residential appraiser and real estate agent, so my natural starting point was residential, 1- to 4-family properties. I have since gone on to get my certified general appraisal license and was the multifamily specialist at my appraisal firm, so my natural progression would be to next invest in multifamily. You will have a natural advantage due to your experience that those who are inexperienced won't have. Start there.

Instead of reinventing the wheel, try to make your business in that niche better than your competition. You will save yourself much frustration and money and be on your path to success in a much quicker manner. By all means, be creative and add your own flavor to what you do, but do so in a way that is well thought out and based on data indicating that your approach has worked for others in some form or fashion.

Look for Other Successful Investors and Do What They Did

"Ninety percent of all millionaires become so through owning real estate. More money has been made in real estate than in all industrial investments combined. The wise young man or wage earner of today invests his money in real estate."

—Andrew Carnegie

Real estate is a proven path to building wealth over the long run. Follow the roadmap those successful pioneers have blazed ahead of you, and you will also experience success. Realize that as you follow the path blazed for you, it is still by far the road less traveled. Most people spend more than they make and invest in things going down in value yielding no income. You will do the opposite and be on a path only the few have explored. And take joy in your journey; the financial freedom will be great, but stop to view the beautiful vistas along the road less traveled—they are just as rewarding. Yes, the road may be a bit bumpy and feel more isolated at times—this is a testimony to you being on the road less traveled. The easier path is paved but doesn't lead where you are going. And remember—the journey is the story— the destination isn't. The story is what you will tell your grandkids.

Get Rich Quick Doesn't Work

*"Get rich quick schemes are for the lazy and unambitious.
Respect your dreams enough to pay the full price for them."*

—Dr. Steve Maraboli

Be warned—those who promise a quick fortune through real estate investing are not to be trusted. While there is the occasional story of a real estate investor who made a lot of money in a short period of time, it is the exception, not the rule. The successful real estate investors I know made their wealth over a long period of time by making good decisions day in and day out, and not by chasing unattainable returns. Pigs get fat; hogs get slaughtered.

Work On Your Business,
Not In Your Business

*"Most entrepreneurs fail because you are working IN
your business, rather than ON your business."*

—Michael Gerber, *EMyth Revisited*

Go to work *on* your business, not *in* your business. Focus on building systems that can run without you, not a job that requires your constant attention. Think Chick-fil-A, McDonalds, etc. They have this nailed down—no need to reinvent the wheel as a franchisee—follow the system, and it works like a charm. If you want to achieve scale in your real estate business and experience freedom with your time, you must focus on this principle. Most people go into real estate to achieve financial freedom and to spend time with ones they love doing things they enjoy and are passionate about. Make sure you don't fall victim to trading one job for another, or worse, ending up with two full-time jobs and even less time for meaningful things.

Real Estate Done Right Will Bring Great Wealth over Time

"Real estate cannot be lost or stolen, nor can it be carried away. Purchased with common sense, paid for in full, and managed with reasonable care, it is about the safest investment in the world."

—Franklin D. Roosevelt

FDR had it right. Real estate can't be lost, stolen, or carried away. Buy it, manage it well, and hang on to it until it is paid in full. You will create true wealth if you can execute this plan. Many before you have done so, and the results have been extraordinary. Give it a shot.

Hold on for the Ride

"Buy on the fringe and wait. Buy land near a growing city. Buy real estate when other people want to sell. Hold what you buy."

—John Jacob Astor

Buying real estate on the fringe of a good city with current job growth and population growth is a great buy-and-hold strategy. Many times properties in the heart of a great city are already too expensive to hold long term for cash flow purposes, but fringe properties are still affordable. As the city continues to expand economically and experience population growth, it will grow into its fringe areas, and you will often experience outsized annual appreciation rates and returns.

Land Has Much Utility

"Buy land, they're not making it anymore."

—Mark Twain

Land can be a wonderful investment but carries with it a different set of criteria than your typical single-family home. Most land is not income producing and is invested in with the plan of development or speculation that prices will rise, and a profit be made. Buying and developing land in a great market is a strategy some have used to build their real estate empire. Whether it be commercial development, developing raw land into a subdivision, or utilizing the land in a ground lease structure, there are many creative ways to monetize land development.

Investopedia defines a ground lease as follows:

A ground lease is an agreement in which a tenant is permitted to develop a piece of property during the lease period, after which the land and all improvements are turned over to the property owner. A ground lease indicates that the improvements will be owned by the property owner unless an exception is created and stipulates that all relevant taxes incurred during the lease period will be paid by the tenant. Because a ground lease allows the landlord to assume all improvements once the lease term expires, the landlord may sell the property at a higher rate.

Stay Humble

*"You have to break free of your past to discover yourself
and you have to discover yourself to create a future."*

—Michael Gerber

You can't create a successful real estate business thinking about the deal that got away, the job you lost, or what might have been. You must keep your head in the game, and you have to separate yourself emotionally from the roller-coaster ride of life and real estate investing, and adopt a stoic mind-set toward your experiences, both good and bad.

Knock one out of the park? "I am blessed by God and am fortunate."

Experience a loss? "I learned a ton and will do better next time. God doesn't promise fame and fortune."

You win either way. With this mentality, you will make it through the hottest fire and come out a newly forged steel. And if the joy is in the journey, sit back and enjoy the ride. No one makes it out alive anyway.

Make Money While You Sleep

"Landlords grow rich in their sleep without
working, risking, or economizing."

—John Stuart Mill

My first place of real employment was Subway as a "sandwich artist." And boy did I create some art and bring home the bacon! I remember working 40 hours one pay period and after all deductions, taking home a $200 paycheck. Even then, I couldn't believe how little money I was making for my time and effort.

How about a better idea—how about making money while we sleep, instead?

Real estate is a beautiful thing. If you take care of it and position it to do its job, it will work for you 24 hours a day, 7 days a week. Rain, snow, or shine, it is there working. Night or day it is plugging away, earning you money to pay down your debt, fix any property issues, and hopefully have some left over to put in your pocket. You need to build your army of property soldiers to go out and fight for you 24/7. Your properties will be at war, fighting on your behalf with unending fervor, bringing home the spoils while you lay in bed. Beats $200 a week at Subway.

Never Count Anyone Out

"You can never tell the luck of a lousy calf."

—O'Neil Smelser

I heard this line from my grandfather throughout my childhood as we worked together on the farm.

We would come across a calf misbehaving or looking a bit smaller than the rest, and Grandfather would say, "You can never tell the luck of a lousy calf."

I thought about it a lot then, and I still do today. It's very powerful.

Don't write anyone off—ever. Don't look at what they wear, their skin color, their hair, how they dress, what they drive, where they live, what languages they speak or don't speak, and don't assume you know what they can or can't do.

In real estate, success comes in all shapes and sizes, and more often than not, those that look successful are not actually successful and vice versa. I can't tell you how many real estate millionaires I have talked to that buy their clothes at Walmart or Goodwill and drive paid for cars with over 100,000 miles on them. That is part of the reason for their success—they prioritized investing in the development of their business over investing in impressing others. Don't ever write people off or assume you know their potential.

Your Real Estate System Needs People to Stay Optimized

"To be successful in real estate, you must always and consistently put your clients' best interests first. When you do, your personal needs will be realized beyond your greatest expectations."

—Anthony Hitt

The customer is king, especially in real estate. This doesn't mean that a complaining tenant gets everything they ask for, but it does mean that investment real estate is a customer service business. You own a small machine that needs systems run by people to pump out cash flow. Without the people, the machine pumps out nothing. If you must have people to optimize the machine, get the very best people you can in both your systems and your properties and try to keep them happy.

For example—on a typical rental, approximately 10% is budgeted for vacancy which will vary depending on your market. If the potential gross income for the year (or PGI) is $12,000 for a rental unit (the revenue if each unit was fully occupied all year), the rental cost of losing a tenant is at least $1,200 or $12,000 x 10%. But that doesn't include costs to locate and screen new tenants, utilities for a vacant unit, cleaning, and make ready expenses, etc. Losing a tenant is expensive and creates inertia in your business. Many landlords raise rent gradually or not at all if they have found a great tenant in order to avoid these costs. When comparing scenarios, many times it makes much more financial and emotional sense to keep a great tenant at a slightly smaller rent than could normally be obtained. Of course, always run your numbers and make the smart decision based on your scenario.

You Can Understand Real Estate Investing

"Risk comes from not knowing what you are doing.
Never invest in a business you cannot understand."

—Warren Buffett

Most people invest surplus income in a retirement account or in the stock market while paying very little attention to the underlying assets they are betting their retirement and future livelihood on. This is lunacy. Would you sign up today to take a job in 30 years without researching the future employer to know what their track record is and what is to be expected? Never! Yet most do much worse. They bet the farm on something they don't understand *at all*.

Tamir Sapir said it best, "If you're not going to put money in real estate, where else?"

I concur. Real estate is not rocket science and is something you can understand. The principles are solid and can be learned.

My principles are as follows:

1. Own properties with a margin of safety (margin of safety can be via equity created through value add, equity through down payment, equity through discount to market value from purchase, or through some combination of these).
2. Make sure rental income will cover all operating expenses, including management, as well as your debt payment with good money left over each month. Know your operating expenses going in. Positive cash flow is key.

3. Own properties in areas that show good reason for future price appreciation over time. Don't own in areas trending downward in value without substantial information indicating a turnaround is likely.
4. Hang on for the long run.

Why bet the farm on a business you have zero control over through the stock market? The CEO of that business could decide to dilute the shareholders tomorrow through a new stock issue, and you are left with less. The CEO could make poor investment decisions, or the company could lose favor with the market overnight through no fault of your own. I want you to have more control over your future—own real estate, run it like a business, and hang on to it. Your experience will very likely be the same as those successful investors before you.

Know the Real Estate Market Cycles

"A funny thing happens in real estate. When it comes back, it comes back up like gangbusters."

—Barbara Corcoran

Treat the real estate market as a living, breathing organism. This organism has cycles in its lifeblood. These cycles are as follows:

1. Recovery
2. Expansion
3. Oversupply
4. Recession

It behooves you as an investor to know where you are today in this cycle. Each phase can go on for years, so it is up to you to do your due diligence. Those who bought investment real estate with no equity using 100% financing from 2005–2007 lost perspective on the market cycles and paid the price for it through financial distress in 2008.

A beautiful thing about a cycle is that it is predictable. When you go through the next real estate recession, load the truck on quality rental properties at discount prices. The market will come back like gangbusters, and you will reap the reward.

Real Estate Is a Canvas on Which You Can Paint

"Some people look for a beautiful place.
Others make a place beautiful."

—Hazrat Inayat Khan

I love real estate because it gives me a canvas on which to paint. You can be as creative as you want to be with your properties and take pride in looking at the finished product when you are done. Real estate investors have the ability to touch a community in a way few do by beautifying the real estate properties they work with. Don't be the landlord who runs the roach infested property that is falling apart with no plans for positive change. Be the landlord that views your tenants as people in need of a great place to live. This doesn't mean spend money in excess—but don't be a Scrooge with your money, either. You can't take it with you. A well-maintained property will attract and keep good tenants, and your reputation as an investor will benefit as well.

Time is Your Most Precious Resource

"Don't simply trade your time for money. Trade your time for assets that will compound and return your money, thus buying you more freedom with your time."

—my perspective

Freedom with your time is the definition of true wealth. Don't just work a job to get cash. You have a finite amount of time on this earth, and if asked, I don't think anyone would outright admit that they are willing to trade the days from now until death for a certain amount of cash. If that is the case, use your time to purchase assets that compound your initial investment and return even more money, which buys you freedom with your time away from the grind. Use that time to enjoy your life with family, friends, and honoring God through making the world a better place and helping others. Keep what is important, important. Don't just trade your time for money to purchase crap that will end up being donated to Goodwill. Your time is your most precious resource and won't be given back. Use it wisely.

Focus on Acquiring a Great Property at a Fair Price

"It's far better to buy a wonderful company at a fair price, than a fair company at a wonderful price."

—Warren Buffett

You are far better off owning great investment properties that you purchased at a fair price than you are owning fair properties you purchased at a great price, excluding extreme examples, of course. Set your cash flow goals as your line in the sand, then go and try to buy these properties in the very best markets and locations you can. My partner and I aim for $100 net profit per door per month on multifamily properties and $200 net profit per month on single-family properties, and this is after all operating expenses and debt payment. We chose to build our portfolio in growing areas such as Huntsville, Alabama, and Fort Worth, Texas, due to the population and economic growth projections coupled with the availability of properties at the price point we were seeking.

Don't settle for reaching your profit goal through by buying a bad property in a bad market. Try to find the very best market you can and try to achieve this profit goal there—you will experience fewer headaches with the management of the property, have a higher quality tenant, and realize better appreciation on your asset's property value. Your chances of holding the asset long term are also higher. Think of cash flow as your cake and appreciation as your icing. You don't want cake with no icing, and you don't want icing with no cake. You want plenty of both. And have patience—in this game, you can have your cake and eat it, too.

Making Mistakes Indicates Learning—Embrace Them

"In school we learn that mistakes are bad, and we are punished for making them. Yet, if you look at the way humans are designed to learn, we learn by making mistakes. We learn to walk by falling down. If we never fell down, we would never walk."

—Robert T. Kiyosaki, *Rich Dad, Poor Dad*

You must open yourself up to making mistakes to be successful in real estate. The key is never making a mistake that can put you out of the game. Never bet the farm and take on a risk that if incurred, would wipe you out. You will learn through mistakes, and people will doubt you as they watch you fail. This is a sign you are on the right track. If no one doubts you, you are likely not being bold enough in your endeavors. The status quo loves to doubt someone as they try to break away, and then say, "I told you so," when you have reached the top. Ignore them from start to finish, and you will be able to focus more on achieving what you set out to achieve. Don't do it for fame and fortune, but to make the world a better place. This will keep you honest and humble. And remember, you are only a phone call away from calamity. Stay humble.

Failure Equals Learning and Learning Equals Progress

"This is one of the most important lessons of the scientific method— if you cannot fail, you cannot learn."

—Eric Ries, *The Lean Startup*

How do you turn an idea into a business? Test. Receive results. Analyze the results. Iterate. Repeat. This is also how you build your real estate business. Test what you believe to work. Observe the results. Analyze the results for patterns. Tweak the variables and retest. Once your tests are yielding the results you seek, pour on the gasoline. Don't go too fast before you have had time to prove your business model. Validate your hypothesis through testing and data, then scale.

Achieve Economies of Scale

*"In order to experience the benefits diversification in
real estate provides, you must achieve economies of
scale, preferably as quickly as economically possible."*

—my perspective

If you own only one single-family rental and have the tenant move
out, you experience a 100% vacancy rate in your portfolio. No cash
flow, but the payments for utilities, insurance, taxes, and maintenance
are still rolling in. This risk needs to be diversified away as quickly as
possible. You wouldn't put all your money in only one stock, would
you? Don't invest all your money into only one property, unless that
property carries diversification through multiple units. Even then, the
more multiunit properties you own in different locations, the more
your risk is diversified.

Multiple unit investing can be achieved through investing in apartments, mobile home parks, self storage units, retail strip centers, etc.
The quicker you can move away from single-family investing into these
areas, the quicker you can scale and create mind-blowing generational
wealth. Owning multiple single-family investment properties works
as well, but the inertia to scaling is much greater.

Educate Yourself and Then Take Massive Action

"Intellect without will is worthless, will without intellect is dangerous."

—Sun Tzu

It won't help you build a real estate business to read every real estate book and listen to every real estate podcast, and never make an offer on a property. On the flip side, it will do a great deal of damage to go hard charging in and making rash decisions with large sums of money and debt, with no knowledge of what you are doing. You need both.

Seek mentorship from someone who is truly willing and able to mentor. Read every book you can. Listen to podcasts. Go to real estate meetings. Join real estate groups. Tag along with investors doing deals so you can learn. Once you have educated yourself on the process, don't be afraid to pull the trigger on your first deal. Make sure you start on a deal that if you are off, it won't put you out of the game.

Remember—success is great, and failure (within a certain scale) is learning. You can't lose either way.

Observe What Is Working and Repeat It

"The goal of Customer Development is not to avoid spending money but to preserve cash while searching for the repeatable and scalable business model. Once found, then spend like there's no tomorrow."

—Steve Blank, *The Startup Owner's Manual*

You must identify your business model before you build your business. You don't have to reinvent the wheel, but you can get as creative as you want. Want to build a single-family buy-and-hold portfolio? Want to own apartments? Want to develop class A office space? Great. What is your deal criteria? How much cash flow do you need after expenses and debt service? How will you handle management? How will you source deals? Do you reinvest profits? What are your cash-on-cash (COC) metrics? What markets will you invest in? How will you finance the properties? Who will handle construction/rehab? Who can you learn from that has done this before you *and experienced success?* These seem like basic questions, but many investors strike out without having the first clue on any of these. And many of those investors experience a failure they don't come back from. You can avoid that.

Find your repeatable, scalable business model, and then spend your money to grow your real estate business. You can do it, but it won't be easy.

Plans That Go Unexecuted Are Worthless

"Everyone can be spreadsheet millionaires,
but in reality, it takes a team on the ground
to execute what is in the spreadsheet."

—Joe Fairless

How many times do we build our plan in a spreadsheet and get excited about what our plan can and will produce? The danger is being a spreadsheet millionaire only, and not taking action. You must build out systems by forming your team to make this dream a reality. Turn that spreadsheet million into a real million by taking action and building your crew. No one can do it alone. That doesn't mean you need to hire a bunch of people; in fact, many build their team through adding independent contracts who are all-stars in their field.

All-star team members you need:

- Brokers/agents specializing in your property type
- Financing pro (hard money, private money, banker, mortgage broker, etc)
- Insurance agent
- Attorney specializing in real estate
- Contractor/contractor crew
- Property manager
- Accountant specializing in real estate

The Opportunity Is There in Real Estate

*"I believe that if you've determined to make a better
life for yourself and your loved ones through real
estate, the opportunity is there for the taking."*

—Brian Murray, *Crushing It In Apartments
and Commercial Real Estate*

Drama reigns supreme in the stock market—that is why they have 24-hour-a-day shows dedicated to watching its every tick in local and international markets. Notice there isn't a 24-hour-a-day station devoted to buying and holding income producing real estate? That is because it is boring. And boring gets the job done. Sure, we have some real estate options on TV, but they typically cover the speculative end of real estate (flipping). Building a long-term portfolio of cash-flow positive properties isn't nearly as sexy to watch, because it takes place over years, not days.

Minimize drama in your life. Invest in hard assets that will pay you to hold on to them while you wait for them to increase in value. You will be thanking yourself years down the road.

Real Estate Will Pay You While It Goes up in Value

"Now one thing I tell everyone is learn about real estate. Repeat after me, 'real estate provides the highest returns, the greatest values, and the least risk.'"

—Armstrong Williams

My first investment property was a shocking experience. I closed on a duplex in a great area of Dallas. My family would live in the 3 bed/2 bath unit while we rented out the 2 bed/1 bath unit next door. I used an FHA loan to buy the property, which allowed me to put only 3.5% down on the purchase since it would be owner-occupied. The area had been appreciating at above 5 percent for the last few years with no signs of slowing down. After signing the closing docs, I received the deposit check as well as next month's rent for the 2 bed, 1 bath occupied unit. The money I received from the rented unit next door nearly covered the entire mortgage payment. This seemed like a dream I didn't want to wake up from.

"Why does everyone not do this? And do they know it is possible?" I wondered.

You mean that someone else will pay down my debt on the property as I live for free in the other unit while the property compounds in value every year at around 5%? And I only put 3.5% down to buy this?

Real estate is amazing. Someone will live in the asset you purchased *and pay it off for you while it goes up in value.* Your income is sheltered by depreciation, which, if need be, can be accelerated to maximize tax savings (talk to your CPA about this). And then your rental income is taxed at the lowest tax rates. If you decide to do a cash-out refi on your property, it is also done tax free. A truly beautiful thing! Take advantage of all these benefits by building your own real estate portfolio.

Find Balance and Chase Your Dreams

"There are 1,440 minutes in each day. That is the one common denominator we all share. With respect to time, we are all on equal footing. And most people, rich or poor, use about 1,200 of those minutes for the following activities: work, commuting, family-related, sleeping, eating, bathing, bathroom, grooming and dressing. That leaves about 240 minutes of time each day. And it is what the rich do with those 240 minutes that separates them from everyone else."

—Tom Corley, *Change Your Habits Change Your Life*

Tom Corley's research shows that the wealthy use their 240 minutes in the following ways:

1. Take time every day to dream and work on that dream.
2. Take time every day to develop yourself through practice and learning.
3. Exercise daily taking care of the body, mind, and spirit.
4. Build and nourish relationships every day.
5. Take time to relax and enjoy life every day.

Balance is crucial in our lives, and Tom Corley shows this through his research of the wealthy. If you want to achieve the success of the ultra-successful you admire, you must adapt the habits that lead to their success. And much more important than building wealth is taking care of relationships in your life as well as your own mind, body, and spirit. Your legacy will be built on how you treated people, the way you achieved your achievements, and the character you showed in the process. Don't sacrifice any of these to build wealth.

Opportunity Cost Can
Not Be Ignored

*"An investor should act as though he had a lifetime
decision card with just twenty punches on it."*

—Warren Buffett

This is phenomenal advice to apply to real estate investing. Pretend
you get only 20 punches on your real estate purchase punch card, and
then you can't buy any more. What would you purchase to build you
real estate portfolio? For me, I want the quality properties with large
scale, allowing me the greatest opportunity for wealth creation. This
naturally pushes one away from speculation and towards achieving
scale through purchasing large stabilized properties at a fair price
with value add potential. Choose like you can only buy 20, and your
experience will be much better. You don't need to limit your portfolio
to only 20 deals, but the concept still applies.

Keep Perspective and Grind Through

*"Life is about perspective and how you look at
something. Ultimately, you have to zoom out."*

—Whitney Wolfe

A year into our real estate investing journey my business partner and I
hit a low point. A few of our properties were taking longer than anticipated to sell and rent, and things weren't going exactly as planned. To
boot, our goal was to receive all of our investment capital back after
our refinances, and we had left some of our investment capital locked
in our properties. We felt like the sky was falling.

Then I went home and wrote down exactly what we had accomplished over the last 12 months to put things in perspective. We now
owned $3 million in high quality renovated and cash flowing real
estate in A and B class areas and had invested $225,000, a mere 7.5%
of the overall portfolio value. We now had $900,000 in equity in our
portfolio—a whopping 4X on our initial $225,000 investment.

I asked myself, "Would the average investor be happy to turn
$225,000 into $900,000 in 12 months?"

The answer was a resounding yes! In fact, millions invest much
more to receive drastically less. I needed to zoom out and have perspective on our success, even though in the moment, we didn't *feel* successful. We talked with a lender and discovered we could refinance our
portfolio at 80% loan-to-value and receive our entire initial $225,000
investment back!

Take time to zoom out and see the progress you have made overall. Don't let a few bumps in the road dampen your spirit or derail you from pursuing your goals. The real estate race is a marathon, not a sprint. Look at the miles you have behind you, what you have accomplished, and take courage!

Persistence Is Key

"Nothing in this world can take the place of persistence. Talent will not—nothing is more common than unsuccessful men with talent. Genius will not—unrewarded genius is almost a proverb. Education will not—the world is full of educated derelicts. Persistence and determination alone are omnipotent."

—Calvin Coolidge

Through all my reading, life experiences, and discussion with successful real estate investors, there is one thing essential to achieving your real estate investing goals—persistence. Persistence through adversity, persistence towards your goals, a willingness to fail forward, a willingness to learn and tweak the process as you go, and a grit to never give up.

Want to buy your first rental property? Persistence. Can't find a lender to fund your deal? Persistence. Have a property that just won't sell? Persistence. Trying to get a license in your field? Persistence. Bad tenants trash your property? Persistence. Want to flip 10 houses a year? Persistence. Want to flip 10 houses a month? Persistence. Want your investment properties to pay your kids' way through college? Persistence. Want to transition from owning single-family to owning apartments? Persistence. Want to own a billion dollars in investment real estate? Persistence. Want your real estate portfolio to create enough passive income to quit your job? Persistence.

You Will Get Better as You Go—Don't Stop

"Formal education will make you a living; self-education will make you a fortune."

—Jim Rohn

I was formally a college professor of finance and real estate, so you know that this quote rings true if I included it. As a college student, I dreamed of owning my own real estate investment properties and building my own investment real estate business, but no college courses taught me how to do this. The real estate text books gave me tons of definitions and a few lessons on operating statements, but the heart and soul were missing. It was not until I purchased my first property that I learned about being a real estate investor. When I taught Real Estate on the college level, I took that opportunity to teach my students how to invest in real estate.

You must self-educate to become a successful real estate investor. Many of the gurus are simply trying to sell courses and have sugar coated their message to the point that it is impotent. Roll up your sleeves and learn through experience. Terrified to start? It is normal to be scared on your first deal. How about finding an investor in your area and doing a partnership with them in order for you to learn? Don't like partnerships? Offer to help do work on the deal to simply sit in on all the details, even if you don't get ownership.

Self-education is how the icons in their field achieved their success. Think Eminem took a class on how to rap? Did Jordan just go to basketball camps? Did Lincoln take a course on how to become a great U.S. president? Did Robert Kiyosaki just take classes on real estate investing? No. They all immersed themselves in their craft; and through years of hard work, dedication, and determination, the cream rose to the top.

Think for Yourself

"A lot of people in our industry haven't had very diverse experiences. So they don't have enough dots to connect, and they end up with very linear solutions without a broad perspective on the problem. The broader one's understanding of the human experience, the better design we will have."

—Steve Jobs

If there was one person who connected the dots to see the big picture, it was Steve Jobs. Take the wisdom Steve Jobs gives us and gain a broad understanding of the human experience, and then apply it creatively to your business. Don't be one-sided. Don't do things just because that is the way it has always been done. In fact, when you sense that is the case, look for ways to simplify and innovate.

Collecting rent? Try using an app to streamline things for your tenants as well as other landlords and tenants. Screening tenants? Try thinking through what is currently done to find a way to improve the process for both parties. Trying to source new property deals? How about training and hiring someone remotely to do this for you? Work *on* your business and not *in* your business (*EMyth*), and do so with a big picture view with broad understanding and application of the human experience. It could be the difference between working in a cubicle for someone else vs creating the next Apple in the real estate industry. The world is your oyster.

There Are Massive Advantages to Investing

"To obtain financial freedom, one must be either a business owner, an investor, or both, generating passive income, particularly on a monthly basis."

—Robert Kiyosaki

Rich Dad Poor Dad is a must read for anyone reading this book. Buy it now, and read it as fast as you can. Then reread it. It set most investors I know on the path to financial freedom through real estate investing, and is one of the first real estate books I read that inspired me on this journey.

In *Rich Dad Poor Dad*, Rich Dad shares the secret to building wealth and unlocking financial freedom in his life with his young apprentice, Robert. Rich Dad teaches his aspiring trainee that to obtain financial freedom, either be a business owner or an investor (or both), and generate passive income on a regular basis. Rich Dad loves investing in real estate for passive income, appreciation, and tax benefits, and also owns businesses that kick off regular cash. Monthly passive income (monthly profit after all expenses and debt service) is a reliable way to build wealth over time.

Other People's Money (OPM)

"Banks do not create money for the public good.
They are businesses owned by private shareholders.
Their purpose is to make a profit."

—John Rogers

Borrowing OPM (other people's money) is the way to use leverage to grow your real estate business, and banks are one of the many options. One could certainly save enough money over time to pay for all properties in cash, but it would take the average person a lifetime of savings to purchase a handful of properties, and this would not use the greatest wealth creating tool readily available through real estate—leverage.

Banks are in the business of calculating risk and making loans on their cash reserves that earn income for their shareholders. It is no wonder banks are predominately in the real estate business. Through lending on a stabilized property, the real estate brings predictable repeatable monthly income which decreases risk for both the bank and the borrower. The fact that income is rolling in that more than covers all expenses and debt service is the very reason that banks are in the real estate lending business. Let's examine a bank's loan criteria and see if we can apply it to our deal acquisition criteria.

Banks want to protect their loans by lending money on assets with a margin of safety present (equity), by lending on assets going up in value (real estate), with recurring predictable cash flow (steady monthly payments), to borrowers with good credit and a good prospect of being able to pay the bank back. Apply the same to your acquisition process when shopping for a deal and potential tenants for your property.

- Margin of safety (built in equity) after purchase and renovation (25% or better is my goal)
- Predictable monthly passive income after all expenses including 3rd party management and debt payment
- Screen to find tenants that have a high probability of paying you consistently
- Own properties located in areas that have a high probability of outpacing inflation through appreciation over the next 30 years.

Banks want to make loans on investment properties with a *margin of safety*, or equity, built in. On a typical single-family investment property, a bank will do an investment loan at 75% loan to value. If the property appraises for $100k *after* renovation, the bank will lend up to $75k on the property. In this example, the bank protects themselves but requiring a 25% margin of safety in each loan they make. If the borrower stops making payments and the bank takes the property back through foreclosure, they could sell it quickly by discounting the price to only $75K for this property worth $100k. Savvy investors would likely be fighting over that deal if the property was in good shape. The bank gets all their money back and moves on to make more loans.

Know the Different Ways
Real Estate Makes Money

*"How you make your money is a lot more
important than how much you make."*

—Gary Vaynerchuk

There are four ways that real estate makes you money:

1. Cash flow
2. Appreciation
3. Principal paydown
4. Tax benefits

Cash flow: Money left over after all expenses and debt payments. This is the lifeblood of real estate investing.

Appreciation: Investment real estate going up in value over time. Buy real estate and wait, and this is why. Compound interest is your best friend.

Principal paydown: As your tenants pay you monthly, you pay your debt payments and gain equity in the property. Hold it long enough, and the property will be completely paid off, courtesy of complete strangers.

Tax benefits: On top of getting to write off expenses associated with your investment property, you also get depreciation. Depreciation is a tax write-off the government allows to shelter your property's income from taxes. Residential properties can currently be depreciated over 27.5 years and commercial properties over 39 years (minus the land). There is another depreciation option called cost segregation that allows you to front load or accelerate your depreciation to maximize tax savings. Talk to your CPA about what might be the best route for you to take to maximize tax savings over the long run.

Keep a Healthy Balance with All Things

"Work is a rubber ball. If you drop it, it will bounce back. The other four balls—family, health, friends, integrity— are made of glass. If you drop one of these, it will be irrevocably scuffed, nicked, perhaps even shattered."

—Gary Keller, *The One Thing*

Real estate investors are notoriously frugal with an eye ever on the highest and best use of each dollar they have to deploy. If not careful, this pursuit of building an investment portfolio/business can lead to dropping the glass ball of family, friends, health, and integrity. When this glass ball is dropped, many times it breaks and doesn't bounce back. And most real estate investors are working for precisely these things—more time with family, more time with friends, good health, etc. Make sure to keep a healthy balance of pursuing your goals with reckless abandon while keeping the fragile and important things as top priorities. Remember someone who really impacted your life in a positive way? Do the same for your friends, family, and real estate relationships.

The BRRRR Strategy Is a Great Way to Build Your Portfolio

The BRRRR Strategy – Buy, Rehab, Rent, Refinance, Repeat
—Brandon Turner, *Bigger Pockets*

The "BRRRR Strategy" is a phrase coined by Brandon Turner, author of *Bigger Pockets*. BRRRR stands for Buy Rehab Rent Refinance Repeat. Many have used this process to great success, and it is my favorite approach to real estate investing.

The beauty of using the BRRRR strategy is taking control of a property (typically distressed), renovating the property, renting the property out, refinancing to consolidate the former purchase price, fix-up costs, holding costs, refinance costs, and refund of the initial equity investment, and then repeating the process again. The goal is to end up owning a renovated cash flow property with 20% equity or more *with none of your own money invested*. This is getting properties on the house, and with none of your own money invested, you are receiving an infinite return on investment. Beat that!

The key to the BRRR strategy is properly nailing your numbers on the front in. You must nail after repair value (ARV), renovation costs, financing costs, and holding costs, and you must buy the property for the right price to make all this work. You can do it!

BRRRR Strategy Sticking Points

"All your ideas may be solid or even good, but you have
to actually execute on them for them to matter."

—Gary Vaynerchuk

The "BRRRR strategy" is my favorite way to approach real estate investing. This phrase was coined by Brandon Turner of Bigger Pockets as
a shorthand way of naming a practical strategy that has been around
for quite some time. Countless investors have used this method to
go from zero to massive real estate portfolios. The BRRRR acronym
stands for "Buy, Rehab, Rent, Refinance, Repeat." The beauty of this
strategy is that it lends itself to taking control of a distressed property,
repairing it, getting it rented out, and then refinancing to get your
initial investment back (or at least a good chunk of it), which you can
then use to repeat the process.

The top four ways your BRRRR strategy could get hung up, and
what the solutions are:

1. The appraisal comes in lower than anticipated
   a. After you have finished your renovation and the property
      is rented, you start your refinance. If the appraisal comes
      in lower than you'd anticipated, it causes the total loan
      amount to be lower, and requires you to leave some of
      your capital in the deal.
   b. Solution: have some cash reserves and anticipate some
      properties appraising lower than expected. Over the
      long term, your equity is still in the property and your

investment capital locked into the deal is working hard for you.

2. Underestimating your costs

   a. You walk through the property and make an educated guess at repairs without a contractor's or inspector's walk-though and opinion. Once you're in the middle of the renovation process, you realize that you underestimated your repair costs. You end up putting more capital into the deal than you'd budgeted for, and you don't fully recover that extra capital on the refinance portion of your BRRRR.

   b. Solution: Always have a contractor and/or inspector help you generate a realistic estimate for your repair costs.

3. Being too optimistic about a property's comparable value

   a. Because you are excited about a potential deal, you breeze through comparable sales or look at them through rose-colored glasses. Maybe you receive them from a wholesaler and don't double-check, or maybe you have "deal fever" and ignore comps closer to your property in favor of those further away. Either way, the market ultimately determines your property's value, and your error will come back to bite you on your refinance.

   b. Solution: trust your gut but verify it with facts. Always do your homework, and start by figuring out the accurate information on the property itself. Is the advertised square footage correct? Is the current property condition as advertised? How much will taxes increase if you buy the deal? Next, *nail down your comps*. Pull comps closest to your property that are most similar to it. If your property is in a distinct neighborhood, start with your neighborhood. If it is not, look for general boundaries (major roads nearby, for instance). Then take the value you come up with and have a couple other people do the same (another agent, a partner, or an appraiser). If all three of you come up with just about the same value, you have some level of assurance you are in the right ballpark with your estimate. *Tip*: you can hire an appraiser for a few hundred bucks to do a desktop appraisal and give you a written value on the property as if it were renovated. This investment may save you from overpaying for the deal.

4. Doing a loan-to-cost deal instead of a loan-to-value deal

   a. Lenders can be quite crafty when selling their loan services. Our company once dealt with a lender who told us they would do our loan based off of 75% loan-to-value, or a loan for 75% of appraised value. Our property appraised perfectly where we had anticipated, and we were going to receive all of our initial cash back upon our cash-out refinance. We received the HUD closing statement one day prior to closing, and noticed that $45k of our capital was not being returned. When I called the loan officer, he admitted to making a mistake and said that they could only do a 75% *loan-to-cost* loan for us. Loan-to-cost is much different than loan-to-value in that loan-to-cost is solely based off of your project costs and completely ignores the property's appraised value (assuming it is higher than purchase price + costs). We were out of time to find another lender, so the slip-up required a massive chunk of our capital to be locked into the deal.

   b. Solution: Make sure the lender understands and is on board with your strategy of refinancing to recover your capital based on the property's loan-to-value. Then, get the lender's agreement to do a loan-to-value (and not loan-to-cost) loan in writing.

In conclusion, the BRRRR strategy is my favorite way to build a real estate portfolio. The strategy works on all property types as the fundamental principles are the same—buy, rehab, rent, refinance, repeat. Beware of the potential pitfalls listed above, and you will have a higher change of success with your BRRRR.

Today's Learning Tip:
Cap Rate: Net Operating Income/Value
A cap rate is used by investors to both value a property as well as compare a property's performance with that of its peers.
Example: An apartment complex with a yearly NOI of $100k is for sale for $1,000,000 = 10% cap rate.

Live Your Passion

"Live your passion. What does that mean, anyway? It means that when you get up for work every morning, every single morning, you are pumped because you get to talk about, or work, with or do the thing that interests you the most in the world. You don't live for vacations because you don't need a break from what you're doing—working, playing, and relaxing are one and the same. You don't even pay attention to how many hours you're working because to you, it's not really work. You're making money, but you'd do whatever it is you're doing for free."

—Gary Vaynerchuk, *Crush It! Why Now Is the Time to Cash In on Your Passion*

Can we make a deal? Look yourself in the mirror, and answer the question: am I living my passion? If you say no, then change! The world needs your God given unique talents in your area of passion. Many times it is the fear of failure (either career or financial) that keeps us from stepping out in faith and pursuing work in our area of passion. But why? What are we so afraid of? Being broke? You came into this world with no clothes on your back and no money in your pocket, and you will leave the same way. Everything you have goes to someone else. Why live in fear? Overcoming this fear will unlock your true potential, and I am cheering for you to make that leap. Get up for work every day pumped to meet the day, feeling like you would do what you are doing for free, and you will absolutely love it. No amount of money is worth missing out on that.

Be Disciplined

*"We don't have to be smarter than the rest. We
have to be more disciplined than the rest."*

—Warren Buffett

Real estate is unique when compared to the stock market or other
investment choices. Real estate has a relatively high switching cost
associated with its sale or purchase. We will call this switching cost
our "discipline fee." Sell after a short holding period, and the discipline
fee is severe. Sell after a long holding period, and the disciple fee is
likely inconsequential.

These switching costs come in the form of closing and financing
costs as well as time involved. In my current market, the average days
on the market for a single-family home sale in the $100k to $300k
range is 90 days. From the time the home is listed, it takes an average
of 3 months to sell. Utilities must be paid, the mortgage must be paid,
the property must be maintained, the property must be marketed,
etc. This high switching cost and inertia is also what makes real estate
investors wealthy and able to capitalize from a rather inefficient market
when compared to a more efficient market such as the stock market.
Where inefficiencies exist, there is money to be made.

Avoid a high discipline fee by holding properties long enough
to experience the benefits. Wealth is accumulated in real estate by
being disciplined and playing the long game, using cash flow to pay
the monthly debt down with a little left over while your asset goes up
in value. If you purchase a home at retail price in move-in condition
and then decide to sell the home 3 months later, it is likely you will
lose money due to switching costs. Appreciation hasn't had time to

work its magic, you haven't had time to pay down the debt, you haven't collected much rent profit, etc. With selling costs including broker fees of 6% and typical closing costs of another 2%, you are looking at around an 8% cost to sell. If you buy a home for $100k and sell for $100k 3 months later, in this scenario you would lose around $8k.

This is a good reason to hang on to a good piece of real estate as long as you can, let it work its magic, and that will minimize the hit that selling the property makes on your overall profit. Let's say instead you hold this property as a rental for 30 years until it is paid off. You buy for $100k putting $20k down on the purchase, it appreciates at 3.5% per year for 30 years, and you then sell for $280k. $280k x .92 (subtract 8% for selling cost) = $258k net (rounded), getting nearly 13x your initial investment. Selling costs don't matter at that point!

Anything Is Possible

*"I learned that if you work hard and creatively, you
can have just about anything you want, but not
everything you want. Maturity is the ability to reject
good alternatives in order to pursue even better ones."*

—Ray Dalio, *Principles*

Anything you want is available (barring physical limitation of course).
The work required to get what you want varies with the wildness of
the dream, but you are capable. Sitting on the couch won't get you
there...taking action will. What can you take action on today that you
will be proud of in five years?

The Execution of a Good Idea Creates the Magic

"Everyone has good ideas, but it is the execution of a good idea that creates the magic."

—Ted Zoller

A college professor once said something I will never forget. "Everyone has good ideas, but it is the execution of a good idea that creates the magic. If you have a good idea and don't plan to act on it, then give it away. You will have more, and maybe someone out there will create something meaningful with your idea that will change the world."

An idea or intention is nothing without a willingness or ability to execute on it, and this is where 99% of people stay; in the idea phase. Paralyzed by choices and options, they dream, but take no action. They lack the maturity to leave good options for the best option. Don't be a statistic; take action on your idea and know that failure is a mark of your progress. Write your goals down with steps to achieve your goals. Once you have your goals written down with steps identified, share your goals with an accountability partner. With enough determination and persistence, your action will lead to success.

Failure and learning is a badge of honor you earn for being unlike than the 99% stuck in idea mode. You have broken away from the pack and are navigating the wild woods on your own. The trail isn't as well worn, and of course you will experience hardship and become flat out exhausted and frustrated at times. But you are making progress that most dream about, and although lonely at times, you will reach higher ground with clear green pastures and a view second to none.

And from that place, down below you will see the millions stuck in idea mode, with the briars and thickets in front of them, afraid to launch out on their journey. Reach out to them one by one, and help them get going on their journey, too.

Thought and Purpose

"In order to accomplish anything, thought
must be wedded to purpose."

—James Allen, *As a Man Thinketh*

Flipping houses to fund the purchase and rehab of buy and hold properties is a great strategy. To optimize the process, you must create a well-oiled machine that runs on efficient systems. Automate every step of the process, from sourcing deals, to the renovation process, to staging your flips, to selling the flips. One piece of this system is what materials will be used on your renovation, and from our above example, a great way to streamline this process is by using the same materials on each job. With detail down to the SKU number and price for each piece of your renovation, you will save money in construction time and holding costs, contractor fees, and make the project easier on all parties involved.

Create a system around each process in your flip and then work on your system until it can operate without you. Look at a large business you admire, and I will bet the founder has done just that.

On Calculating Renovation Costs Quickly

"Luckily, there is another way that is much easier. It's the p/
sq. ft. method but for rehab costs…the figures given next are
what I've seen as a general guideline for contractors. Every
market is different, so don't take these estimates as set in stone.
Clean-Up Rehab: $5 to $10 PSF
Lipstick Rehab: $15 PSF
Full Interior Rehab: $20 PSF
Full Rehab: $25 PSF
Full Rehab including 2 big ticket items
(roof, AC, pool, etc.): $30 PSF
Full Rehab including 3 big ticket items
(roof, AC, pool, etc.): $35 PSF"

—Ryan Pineda, *Flip Your Future*

Ryan is a wise man and gained his wisdom through flipping 100 houses per year and building systems to accomplish his flips. I recommend his book *Flip Your Future* if you are considering flipping.

Typically, if there is an error in calculating renovation costs on a flip, it is made on underestimating costs. Ryan takes the mystery out of the equation by giving you a back of the napkin way to get a general idea of how much your renovation should cost.

Ryan defines these as follows:

- Clean Up Rehab—very light rehab. Includes paint, carpet, and small repairs.

- Lipstick Rehab—paint, tile or laminate flooring, granite countertops, kitchen cabinet refinishing, small bathroom rehab, and light landscaping.
- Full Interior Rehab—replacing everything inside
- Full Rehab—everything from full interior rehab plus a big ticket item or items such as roof, AC, or pool—the more big ticket items included, the more expensive (as seen above).

On top of this, many flippers recommend you build in a 20% overage cushion. For example, I would calculate renovation costs as follows:

1,200 SF home needing a full interior rehab along with new roof and new AC
$30 PSF x 1,200 SF = $36,000
Overage of 20% x $36,000 = $7,200
Total Renovation Budget: $36,000 + $7,200 = $43,200

Remember, You'll Be Gone Soon

"Remembering that I'll be dead soon is the most important tool I've ever encountered to help me make the big choices in life. Because almost everything—all external expectations, all pride, all fear of embarrassment or failure—these things just fall away in the face of death, leaving only what is truly important. Remembering that you are going to die is the best way I know to avoid the trap of thinking you have something to lose. You are already naked. There is no reason not to follow your heart."

—Steve Jobs, Stanford Commencement Speech

This applies not only to real estate, but to life in general. Failure is part of living and part of being successful, especially the kind of success that is admired. For the Michael Jordans, the Thomas Edisons, the Oprahs, the Steve Jobs, the Meryl Streeps, the Elon Musks of the world, these stories have great successes laced with failures along the way. Zoom in and only examine the failure, and you would be missing the amazing successes we all know these icons for. But no one wants to be a failure. While we are failing, we feel strange. People don't get behind us with vigor. People don't engage with us as much in social settings, we get funny looks when we tell people what we are working on, what we are trying to do, because people aren't drawn to someone in the throes of failure, because people are sheep. Drawn to the glitz and glamor, people flock from one Super Bowl MVP to the winner of *Dancing with the Stars* or *The Voice*.

"What phenomenal talent! And to persevere through such adversity! How amazing!" they say.

In each of these stories, I guarantee you, you will find a person who has struggled for years with many failures in reaching their goals, with many doubting them at the very moment they most needed support. Those individuals made the decision to block out the noise, the doubt, the lack of support, and to focus on their goals with reckless abandon. Who cares what others think? Do you think in 200 years it will matter what someone you knew back in college thinks about your new idea? No! Do it because it is the right thing for you to do, whether anyone gets behind it or not. And the funny thing is, if you pursue it long enough with enough passion, with a determination, and keep at it through thick and thin, it will work. And when it does, the same people that doubted you will be standing there cheering saying I knew they could do it! Either way, you're already naked. Remembering that you are going to die is the best way to avoid the trap of thinking you have something to lose. There is no reason not to follow your heart. And know this—you can reach out to me in your failure, and I will support you. I will cheer you on. I will celebrate the fact that you stepped out in faith and tried to do something original in spite of all the inertia. And I will celebrate your day of arrival as well. Just take the first step, then the next, then the next. Love you guys and believe you can do more than you think you are capable of.

10,000 Hours

"In fact, by the age of twenty, the elite performers (violinists) had each totaled ten thousand hours of practice." p. 38

"The emerging picture from such studies is that ten thousand hours of practice is required to achieve the level of mastery associated with being a world-class expert—in anything," writes the neurologist Daniel Levitin. p. 40

"To become a chess grandmaster also seems to take about ten years. (Only the legendary Bobby Fisher got to that elite level in less than that amount of time: it took him nine years.) And what's ten years? Well, it's roughly how long it takes to put in ten thousand hours of hard practice. Ten thousand hours is the magic number of greatness." p. 41

— Malcolm Gladwell, *Outliers*

To become an outlier and take things to the next level, you must put in the time. And put in a lot of time. So what about you, you might ask?

I got my 10,000 hours by becoming an appraiser as well as a real estate agent starting back in 2005. While I appraised homes, duplexes, triplexes, and fourplexes, I also acted as a buyer and sellers' agent for others, as well as an agent on my own deals. I went on to upgrade my appraisal license from residential to commercial, and then spent time as the multifamily specialist at my firm, appraising apartment complexes, mobile home parks, as well as retail, office, land, and special use properties. All the while, I was buying and selling my own investment properties, doing flips, renovating homes, and getting experience. I sold everything just before the market crash in 2008 (pure luck) and went to graduate school. I then launched my own appraisal business as I scaled my investment property business on the side. I also spent 2 years teaching finance and real estate on the college level. Am I incredible? No. Do I think I even come close to knowing it all? Not by a long shot. But I do know that putting in over 10,000 hours at the real estate game has equipped me with a great skill set to build my real estate investment portfolio. I made a ton of mistakes, but have also learned a ton. And that is part of the process.

So what if you don't have any experience and don't own any properties? That's okay! Start in on your 10,000 hours. Read books on how to do this. Listen to podcasts. Watch YouTube videos. Shadow real estate investors in your local community. Take some classes (not from the shister gurus out there) on investing. Get your real estate license or appraisal license. If you are interested in wholesaling, learn from a wholesaler who has been successful and done this for a while. Volunteer to work for someone doing flips for free to learn the process. There are so many ways to get started, but don't sit and do nothing because you don't know what to do. No one knows what to do when they start, and that is part of the journey. I plan to be a lifetime learner in this field, and that is the entire reason I started my podcast The Daily Real Estate Investor. I wanted to share what I have learned, and also share the learning process as I continue to learn, and hopefully that helps you become successful as well.

Invest in Yourself, Then
Invest in Real Estate

"The most important investment you can make is in yourself."

—Warren Buffett

Investing in real estate is secondary to investing in yourself. You must develop the skills necessary to achieve your real estate investment goals. The only way one can do this is by investing in learning. In my experience learning in the classroom is much different than learning through experience. Real estate investing requires time on task, trial and error, trying, failing, and learning from the mistakes. This is investment in yourself. Don't be reckless with your money and your investments, but also know that you must learn to be successful. Buffet nails this on the head. The most important investment one can make is in themselves. Buffet spends hours a day reading in his office by himself, working on improving himself, improving his mind, and it shows in the results he has produced over the last 50 years. Berkshire Hathaway has compounded their annual returns at around 21% a year due to Buffett's rule of investing in himself first. Buffet prioritizes improving his mind and improving his ability to reason and solve problems above financial success or progress. For that reason alone, his results have been extraordinary.

If Buffet can go from zero to billionaire by spending hours a day reading in his office, we know his advice is valid. Spend time learning and investing in yourself before blindly investing in something you don't understand, and your results will also be outsized.

Chase Happiness

"People are chasing cash, not happiness. When you chase money, you're going to lose. You're just going to. Even if you get the money, you're not going to be happy."

—Gary Vaynerchuk

Real estate investors tend to be birds of a distinct feather. Many are hyper focused on where every penny is going, as they should be. We get this way because we run numbers on deals, and when we find one that meets our criteria, we strike. What criteria?

Here are some very common criteria investors use to determine if they are interested in a deal:

- Market location
- Team location (property management, contractors, brokers, etc.)
- Appreciation rates (both historical and projected future)
- Cash on cash return
- Return on investment
- Cap rates
- Equity and debt availability

Investors love finding and doing deals, but at the end of the day, it is extremely important that we remember that cash will not make us whole, fulfill us, or make us find purpose. Cash is simply a scorecard for your performance, and a metric to measure your investing decisions by. And it isn't the only metric that matters. Others might be—how did you treat your tenants? Did you take care of your business partners? Did you watch out for your investors? Did you act ethically? How did people feel after dealing with you?

Don't just chase cash—chase meaning and purpose, and there you will find fulfillment. And having a lot of cash will be a great thing if it is secondary to having purpose and leaving others better than you found them.

Staging Your Property

*"Home staging used to be optional. Today,
it's a necessity in selling a house."*

—Barbara Corcoran

Staging your property before sale is paramount. According to a survey by the National Association of Realtors, every $1 spent on home staging results in an approximate $4 profit, a whopping 400% cash on cash return. To boot, homes that are staged tend to sell quicker as opposed to homes that have not been staged. That translates to cost savings through fewer loan payments (less interest), a generally higher offer price by buyers, and fewer holding costs such as utilities, insurance, property taxes, etc. Typically, as a property sits on the market, a buyer will expect a larger discount to list price. If a property has been on the market for 10 days, it is generally more likely to get an offer closer to list price. If a property sits for 6 months, many more lowball offers start to show up. If your property is still sitting on the market after 12 months, the offers may slow to a trickle even though the price has been reduced, and the offers you do get may still be low ball offers.

The takeaway here is although it may seem costly, home staging can increase the offer price you receive for your property, help sell your home quicker, and even create a bidding war among buyers, which can lead to substantial cost savings. I have had several properties that were staged sell within 24 hours of being listed, and they were priced at the top of my comparable sales comps. Staging works.

Buy Property below Its Intrinsic Value

*"Only repurchase shares of the company if the
shares are selling below their intrinsic value."*

—Warren Buffett

Berkshire Hathaway has been in the process of buying shares of the company stock back.

When asked the question of what their plans were to continue buying shares of company stock back, this was Buffett's answer, "Only repurchase shares of the company if the shares are selling below their intrinsic value. You want to be sure the remaining shareholders are better off after repurchase than they were before the purchase."

The way to accomplish this is by buying the stock for a price below its intrinsic value. Another words, if the stock is worth $200 a share intrinsically, and the price that day is $150, this repurchase would create value for the existing shareholders. How does this concept apply to real estate?

Here's how—real estate should be purchased below its intrinsic value as well. We could use the term ARV or after repair value in exchange for the word in intrinsic in this case. You must buy your asset below its ARV in order for the purchase to make sense. Purchasing below ARV is creating value for the shareholder or the business—your business. As you take control of assets below their market value you create wealth. This, in a nutshell, is what Buffett and Munger have done almost flawlessly throughout their careers. Buffett and Munger also hold these assets which they purchase below intrinsic value for the long run.

The takeaway—know what your property will be worth once your value add strategy is completed and know your numbers well. Only purchase within a margin of safety or below the intrinsic value of the asset.

Cash Is King

"Revenue is vanity, profit is sanity, but cash is king."

—Unknown

Cash is king. One example is when making offers on properties. When buying a property, there will often be multiple offers if the property looks to be a good deal. How can you differentiate yourself from the other offers? Cash on the barrel. A seller sees a cash offer as less risky due to the deal not falling through due to the buyer having issues getting financing from their lender. Cash offers also close much quicker, so this decreases holding costs and time to close. Many times, when a buyer is willing to offer cash for a property, they won't ask for seller concessions or any repairs either. This is also optimal for a buyer. At the end of the day, cash represents lower risk to the seller, and that is something a seller puts a premium on.

So how can I come up with enough cash to buy a deal outright? There are several ways. The most obvious just being save the cash yourself. Outside of that, you could use hard money. Hard money will come along with points charged when you borrow the money (typically at least 2% of the loan amount but this can vary) as well as a higher rate of interest than what you would see through the conventional bank route. Hard money lenders typically require you to have some skin in the game as well, often asking for at least 10% equity from you to go along with their 90%. Another way to come up with cash is simply finding a partner, friends and family, or private money. By private money, I mean nontraditional hard money lenders. There are some that have more cash than they know what to do with, and would be happy to lend you the money short term for a little premium.

Have a game plan when you pitch this idea to friends/family/private lenders as they will certainly not lend money to you if they don't feel comfortable with your chances of success. Above all, armed with cash, you will land more deals.

How to Handle Bidding Wars

"Those are the two best words in English, 'Bidding' and 'war.'"
—Evan Daugherty

Bidding wars are great as a seller, but of course, not so great as a buyer. Here is how to approach a bidding war from the buyer's perspective:

- Know your numbers and never overpay
- Never get emotional
- Be willing to let the deal go if the price gets too high

Follow this process to figure out your max bid and never go above your max bid:

1. Know the condition, current occupancy, and history of your property
2. Know the current market value of the property based on comparable sales
3. Know the current market rent of the property based on comparable rents
4. Know the future market rent of the property once value add is completed based on comparable rents
5. Know the ARV (after repair value) of the property once the value add has been completed
6. Know the costs to complete the value add, including: repair costs, holding costs/financing costs, closing costs, overage cushion, etc.
7. Know what margin of safety you are seeking in the deal (equity after project completion)

To make sure you have the above nailed, you need to know the market trends based on your property type and market location ($ per SF sales for comps, $ per SF rents for comps, cap rates if applicable, occupancy rates, appreciation rates, contractor costs per repair item in your market, market trends etc.)

Once you have the above six, then back into your ceiling offer price.

Let's look at an example with an apartment complex.

- 7% cap rate.
- NOI (net operating income) for our property is $1,000,000
- Repair costs/holding costs/financing costs/cushion costs = $500,000
- Margin we require is 25% equity after project is completed
- Current sales price: $8,500,000

First of all, the current sales price is pretty much irrelevant. We want to know what the highest we can pay for this project is and walk away with our 25% equity after we have completed our value add. We calculate that as follows:

After repair value NOI of $1,000,000/cap rate of.07 = $14,285,714
ARV $14,285,714
Margin of safety 25%
Margin of safety .25 x $14,285,714 = $3,571,528
Maximum debt $14,285,714—3,571,528 = $10,714,286
Maximum debt of $10,714,286—total value add costs $500,000 = $10,214,286
Maximum bid $10,214,286
Current price $8,500,000

In this scenario, I would be willing to pay up to $10,214,286 for this project to achieve my 25% equity on this value add deal. I wouldn't be willing to go beyond that. I would also want to meet or exceed my cash on cash return hurdles, but we won't dive into that here.

The takeaways:

- Back into your numbers
- Stick to your guns
- Don't let someone else overpaying influence your decision making

MRI vs ROI

"It is health that is real wealth and
not pieces of gold and silver."

—Mahatma Gandhi

For the last several months, I have been experiencing some mysterious
health issues. Bloodwork has come back normal, and repeated doctors'
visits have led me next to a neurologist. As I sat in the neurologist
office going over the health issues I have been experiencing (muscle
and nerve), the doctor ordered both an MRI and spinal MRI. Later
that day I had 19 different blood tests done, in an effort to be thor-
ough and figure out what was going on. As I sat in the office while the
nurse took an inordinate amount of blood, the thought popped into
my head, "MRI vs ROI."

At the end of the day, ROI is meaningless when you are getting
MRIs. Your health is your most important asset, and it should always
take precedence over any business transaction or pursuit. I would
much rather you live to be 100 years old and lead a low stress and happy
life while working at a coffee shop than I would you own $1 billion
in real estate and die young, stressed out, overweight, and anxious.

There is a happy median I believe. Find a sustainable path to real
estate investing that allows you to exercise and eat healthy daily, spend
time with your family and friends, and enjoy your hobbies. This will
decrease stress in your life, which will generally prolong your time
on this earth. Figure out a way to reach your real estate growth goals
while never compromising on physical health, family and friends,
and your spiritual health. You will be thankful when you look back
on your life.

How to Wholesale a Home

*"Real estate wholesaling is a unique, short-term strategy
for generating income. It consists of finding properties that
can be acquired at significantly lower market value prices,
controlling them through the use of a purchase and sale
agreement, and then while in contract , or shortly after
closing, finding a buyer willing to purchase your contract."*

—Paul Esajian, *The Real Estate Wholesaling Bible*

Real estate wholesaling is the process of acquiring and controlling a property though a purchase contract at a low price, and while under contract, finding another party to buy the property at a higher price. The true form of arbitrage, the wholesaler is the middle man, and essentially buys low and sells higher.

There are different ways to wholesale, with some wholesalers simply assigning the purchase contract over to a third party buyer for a fee and never truly owning the property. Another wholesaling method is to double close the home. This works by the wholesaler finding a buyer and going under contract with them. At closing, the wholesaler closes on the purchase with the initial seller and then turns around and immediately sells the property to the third party buyer.

Wholesalers use these different methods based on wholesaling laws in their markets, and I have purchased wholesale properties through both. Both routes worked out great for me as the end buyer.

Four keys to become a successful wholesaler:

1. Marketing/lead generation—you must be able to find the best deals.

2. Analytical skills—you must know what the property is worth in current and renovated condition. You must know rents and sales comps. Fail here, and your moneymaker could turn on you quickly.
3. Negotiation skills—you must be able to negotiate a price that works for your seller as well as your future buyer. If you can't do this, don't do the deal.
4. People skills—you must be able to work with people, learn what their pain point is, and solve the problem if possible. A seller generally has a financial problem motivating them to sell. Figure out how to help them work through their pressing issue. Sometimes you must handle these situations with great care, always putting the people first.

How much can you make wholesaling a property? There is a very wide range of possibilities, ranging from large losses to large gains. Many wholesalers I have worked with look to net $10k to $20k at a minimum.

Here is an example wholesale deal:

1. Wholesaler uses direct mail marketing and locates an owner interested in selling
2. Seller's property has an ARV (after repair value) of $175,000
3. Property needs $20k in repairs
4. Owner will sell property for $100k to wholesaler
5. Wholesaler goes under contract with seller for $100k
6. Wholesaler advertises wholesale deal to their network for $125k
7. Wholesaler locates buyer willing to pay $120k
8. Wholesaler closes on purchased of property from seller and then closes on sale to third party buyer. Wholesaler nets

$20k profit ($120k sales to end buyer - $100k purchase from current owner).

9. Third party buyer purchases home for $120k and does repairs of $20k, for a total cost of $140k (not including holding and closing costs). Property's ARV (after repair value) is $175k. Third party buyer refinances property at 80% LTV, and now has a debt of $140k on a property valued at $175k, and receives all of their initial cash investment back from the refinance. Third party buyer rents out the home, collects the monthly profit, and lets his tenants pay off the investment he/she purchased through the BRRRR strategy (buy, rehab, rent, refinance, repeat). Third party buyer contracts wholesaler looking for next deal.

Wholesaling is not for everyone, but for those that can master the process mentioned above, there is good money to be made in wholesaling.

Focus on What Is Important

"The amateur and the addict focus exclusively
on the product and the payoff."

—Steven Pressfield, *Turning Pro*

Reading Turning Pro by Steven Pressfield made a massive impact on my life. Pressfield drives home the point time and again that creating your life's work requires focus on what is important and a fundamental change from amateur to pro. When focus is not on the real goal, we spin our wheels and live in the shadows of what is possible.

Real estate and its payoff is great, but to what end? Focus on living your best life and honoring your faith, family, friends, and health in the process. Create your art as a pro and don't focus exclusively on the payoff.

How to Fund Deals

"If hard work is the key to success, most
people would rather pick the lock."

—Claude McDonald

My partner and I just closed on the purchase of four properties in the last 2 weeks. One was purchased with our cash, one was purchased through a bank, one was purchased using hard money, and one was purchased using private money. Here are the pros/cons and details of each experience:

Cash
Real Terms:
Loan: $112k
Interest rate: none
Closing costs: 1% of loan
Pros: Super easy to close—no preapproval needed, no interest payments, paperwork and closing are a breeze, very low closing costs.
Cons: Your cash is quickly used up, leaving you cash poor for any hiccups in your portfolio and renovation plans. Your cash on cash is driven down the more cash you put in—another words, you aren't using beautiful leverage to amplify those returns. Most people don't want to own their properties in 100% cash from the start, so they must do a refi, which means closing costs on the initial purchase as well as the refinance.

Bank

Real Terms:

Loan: $120k

Interest rate: 6.25%

Closing costs: 2.5% of loan

Pros: Lower interest rate than hard money, can do longer term financing, and typically somewhat lower closing costs as compared to hard money.

Cons: Takes much longer to close than hard money. Closing costs including points, junk fees, and an interest rate that can easily be manipulated by the bankers to their advantage. I have had many bankers tell me one thing on the front end, and once I am several weeks in, they drop the hammer by changing a massive detail. In every instance they have said "my bad," but it is too late for me to start over due to sunk costs.

Hard Money

Real Terms: Loan $111k, interest rate 9.95%, closing costs all in 3% of loan amount

Pros: Close lighting fast (just closed on start to finish in 3 days). Much less vetting than banks for qualifications for the loan—tend to care more about the deal than the borrower. Can be easy to work with if you find the right one. Gives you hope in capitalism and real estate investing.

Cons: Higher interest rates than other options. Higher closing costs/points than other options. Can be awful to work with if you find the wrong one. Some hard money lenders tend to promise one thing and then not deliver or not deliver on time. Before we closed our current deal with our current hard money lender, we used two different hard money lenders that flat out dropped the ball several weeks near closing. Both told us they could do the deal going in and ended up costing us the appraisal fee and a ton of time before discovering they couldn't do the deal. One told us they couldn't finance our deal because we owned the property free and clear—made no sense whatsoever.

Private Money

Real Terms: Loan $200k, interest rate 10.5% blended rate between 1st and 2nd liens, closing costs all in 3% of loan amount

Pros: Lender lending 100% of money for purchase + rehab. Quick close. Can't beat it.

Cons: Higher interest rate than banking option and bumpier ride to closing as private money expertise and lending requirements may vary.

Making Mistakes

*"If you're not making mistakes, then
you're not making decisions."*

—Catherine Cook

There is a parable in the Bible that goes something like this—a shrewd business owner gave 3 employees a different amount of talents (money) to invest.

To the first he gave 5 talents. The first invested their five talents and made 5 more talents, thus totaling 10 talents.

To the second he gave 2 talents. The second invested their 2 talents and returned 2 talents, thus totaling 4 talents.

To the third he gave 1 talent. The third was so scared of losing the talent they had, that they buried it in the ground and returned no extra talents. When their debt was due, they had only the talent that had been given to them.

When the owner returned, to the first and second he said, "Well done!"

To the third he said "You didn't even put the talent in the bank so I could have received interest! I will take your talent away and give it to the first with 5 talents."

Isn't that how life works? It isn't about how many talents you have been given, but how you invest the talents you have been given. Whatever you do, don't bury them in the ground! Making mistakes is a sign that you are going for it, that you are hanging it out there, stepping out in faith. Making mistakes is learning. And no baby knows how to walk from day one—they fall a ton…and then start falling less and less...and one day...they conquer the walking thing. Real estate works the same way.

Make mistakes and learn from the mistakes.

This Road Is Not Complicated but Requires Focus

"Take one simple idea and take it seriously."

—Charlie Munger

For the last few years, as a shareholder of Berkshire Hathaway, I have had the pleasure of attending the annual shareholders meeting. The meeting is called the "Woodstock of Capitalism," and it is truly something to behold. Thousands descend upon Omaha, NE to listen to the Oracle of Omaha (Warren Buffet) and his partner Charlie Munger talk shop. Warren is 89 and Charlie is 92 as I write this, and they haven't lost a step. As they bestow their wisdom upon the masses, they eat peanut brittle and drink Cherry Diet Coke.

Charlie Munger gets a lot less acclaim than Warren Buffet, but make no mistake, the guy is solid gold.

And he delivers again with this advice, "Take one simple idea and take it seriously."

If you take one financial decision seriously in your life, take real estate investing seriously. It is the most reliable and proven way to achieve life changing wealth and financial independence. And not wealth for the sake of wealth, but wealth for the sake of freedom. Freedom from jobs where you don't feel alive, freedom to spend time with your family as you choose, freedom to be yourself.

The power is in the focus. Become hyper focused on one thing—and do it with every fiber of your being. No detail will change your resolve. No bump in the road, no variable change, nothing. Take one simple idea, and take it seriously.

Short Term Rentals

"If you accept the expectations of others, especially negative ones, then you never will change the outcome."

—Michael Jordan

We are all familiar with the short term rental craze of late. Airbnb and VRBO have taken the world by storm. The cool thing about what these companies do is basically compete with hotels for short-term stays. One can rent a room or even a bed in many places, or can rent the entire home for as little as a day, and as long as months. On my podcast titled *The Daily Real Estate Investor* I interviewed a guy who is running a full-time Airbnb business and is making six figures only from the management of the properties, not even including the positive cash flow his properties are kicking off. He operates his Airbnb business from Scottsdale, Arizona and capitalizes on the tourism industry there.

Short term rental factors to consider:

1. The cost of furnishing the units.
2. Management fees are typically higher.
3. Cleaning costs are higher due to frequent turnover.
4. Permits/licenses may be required to operate.
5. A city can change legislation on the legality of short-term rentals overnight.

Many owners of short- term rentals do quite well, but you must learn the ropes before you dive in full scale.

Unethical Behavior

"Wall Street is the only place that people ride to in a Rolls
Royce to get advice from those who take the subway."

—Warren Buffett

One of the shareholders at the annual shareholders meeting asked Buffett and Munger a difficult question regarding the unethical behavior that had occurred at a bank Berkshire owned a significant portion of. Buffett responded—they incentivized the wrong behaviors, and this led to the setting up of fake accounts.

"When you find a problem you must do something about it, and that is where they made a mistake. They didn't take action."

Advice—poorly structured incentives can lead your team towards unethical behavior. Make sure your incentives are structured in such a way that they lead to not only the result you want, but the behavior you want to achieve the result. When you, as a business owner, find out something is leading to bad behavior or is being done in an unethical manner, you must do something about it fast.

Working with Contractors

*"You have competition every day because you set
such high standards for yourself that you have
to go out every day and live up to that."*

—Michael Jordan

Rules for working with contractors:

1. Put everything in writing and have it signed by both parties.
2. Don't hire solely based on price.
3. Get word of mouth referrals for a new contractor you are considering hiring from trusted investor sources who have used the contractor previously.
4. Check in on your renovations often and take plenty of pictures.
5. Look for contractors that try to save you money.
6. Have a price and SKU number for each material to be used.
7. Never give contractors large sums of money up front.
8. Make sure your contractor has proper insurance.
9. Incentivize contractors to be timely in their work by providing a potential bonus if they finish early and penalties if they finish late.
10. If they lie to you, move on.

Model What Works

"Success is walking from failure to failure
with no loss of enthusiasm."

—Winston Churchill

You don't have to recreate the wheel to do something as a great success. Modeling is one of the very best ways to experience great success in your own life. Modeling works by looking at what other successful people in your space or your niche have done and copying what they did to become successful. You can actually experience success in a quicker fashion than they did by avoiding some of the pitfalls that they experienced. They've created a path in a roadmap to success. Follow what they have done, execute as they have, and experience success as they have. I looked at other successful authors of real estate books and studied what they did, and tried to implement the same processes and systems that they did, when writing this book. I looked at other successful real estate investors and tried to model my activities after their experiences of success as well. I did the same thing with my podcast before launching my podcast.

Take time to find someone in your space and your niche that has done exceptionally well and then dive deep into what they did to accomplish that. Modeling your path after theirs will create great results.

Different Ways to Earn Money

*"You will never know true freedom until
you achieve financial freedom."*

—Robert T. Kiyosaki, Rich Dad's Cash Flow Quadrant

Cash Flow Quadrants by Robert Kiyosaki

The book cash flow quadrant by Robert Kiyosaki is a must read. Kiyosaki breaks down the way you make can money into four quadrants of a square. The top left is "E" for employee; this is someone who makes money from having a 9-to-5 job. The bottom left quadrant is "S" for self-employed; this person owns their job. The top right hand quadrant is "B" for business owner; this person owns a system and people work for them. The bottom right hand quadrant is "I" for investor; this person has invested money and makes money work for them. Think about a real estate investment like a single-family property—one puts cash down on the property and the property pays down the debt while also giving surplus cash to the investor. Kiyosaki makes the point that we need to work hard to be in the B and I quadrants as quickly as possible. The beautiful part about the B quadrant (business owner) is that you create a system and other people perform work in that system to provide the owner profit. The beautiful part about the I (investor) quadrant is that your cash is out there working for you which frees up your time. Most people do work in the top left-hand corner of the square in the E quadrant (employee quadrant), where the nine to five comes into play. The problem with staying in the E quadrant solely is that you're limited by your time. Simply trading your time for money as an employee will never really leverage the beautiful aspect of a system utilized in the B quadrant or the passive investment of the I quadrant by putting money into an investment that doesn't require your hand's on management to produce profit. In the I quadrant, it is possible to make money while you sleep.

There is absolutely nothing wrong with being in any certain quadrant and no quadrant is more virtuous than another. I suggest you create a plan to leverage these quadrants to free up your time to do things you're passionate about. If you're in the E quadrant, use the income you're making to invest in the B and I quadrants. Another idea would be if you're in the E quadrant and want to work for yourself one day, then save the income you're making from the E quadrant move into a job in the S quadrant where you're self-employed.

I am currently self-employed and do appraisal work from home. This shift away from the E quadrant created the flexibility to invest time and money into the B and I quadrants. I am able to invest in the B and I quadrants as I create my own brokerage business as well as continue to purchase real estate investments.

The wealthy end up with investments in the B and I quadrants, so focus your attention there if trying to build long-term wealth. Think about Warren Buffett and Berkshire Hathaway—they've taken their cash and purchased cash flow profitable businesses but don't run the business themselves—they purchase the businesses with cash and lets the businesses run themselves, creating time to focus on growing their business of purchasing other businesses. It works the same with investments. Take your cash and buy cash flow investments (properties) which return cash for you to reinvest. This will create wealth and freedom of your time.

Hustling

*"The game has its ups and downs, but you can never
lose focus of your individual goals and you can't
let yourself be beat because of lack of effort."*

—Michael Jordan

Michael Jordan was a competitor obsessed with winning and obsessed with the competitive nature of what he was doing. Jordan was obsessed with being the best. You're lucky that you're in a game where you don't have to retire when your vertical starts slipping. Hone your skills, put in the time and work, and hustle your butt off so you can become the very best.

Real estate investing is basically just hustling. Hustle 24/7 to accomplish your goals. Write down your goals, focus on your goals, dwell on your goals, reread your goals, and every day take action to accomplish your goals. If you aren't hustling, you're not really in the game, and to be the best, you must out hustle everyone around you.

A Game to Be Learned and Played

*"The path is the goal. In other words, finding
your path in life is your goal in life."*

—Robert T. Kiyosaki, *Rich Dad's Cash Flow Quadrant*

Real estate is nothing more than a game to be learned and played. Over the last two months we have closed on $1 million in real estate in high quality areas. On my podcast, *The Daily Real Estate Investor*, I interviewed a gentleman who had acquired roughly 600 doors in apartment complexes over the last two years. What you are capable of achieving is subject to your mind-set towards what is possible and your work ethic towards making the dream a reality.

Don't be fooled by chasing a number of doors, but focus on the amount of value that you're building in your portfolio. Talking about how many doors you own is a vanity metric than means very little. You may have $1 million in real estate in six single-family homes in great areas, or $1 million in real estate in a 30-unit apartment complex. Either way you're making great progress.

Take action by writing down your goals into achievable steps along with a specific date for each step. You will turn around one year from now and discover that you are much further down the line than when you started. I found getting super focused and detailed on small goals allows you to accomplish larger goals. I got very focused and honed in on what I needed to do each week to reach my goal for the month and then made sure my monthly goals were in line with my goals for the year. I have a five-year goal and then break it down into months, which allows me to set my weekly goal. Make sure you make it make a written plan and measure your success. As the saying goes, what gets measured gets managed.

Finding a Mentor

—Robert T. Kiyosaki, *Rich Dad's Cash Flow Quadrant*

I have people contacting me asking if I can mentor them in real estate investing on a regular basis. One reason I started the podcast was to help people learn how to invest in a leveraged way to build wealth and achieve financial freedom. Investors and business people only have a certain amount of time in the day to do business, so it's literally impossible to help everyone as much is each person would desire without doing so in a leveraged form or fashion. Both mentoring and being mentored will provide you great benefit. I suggest you try both at some point.

Here are some tips on locating and landing a mentor which will help you on your way.

1. When seeking a mentor, seek first to add value. Volunteer to work for free for a while just to get to know the lay of the land and learn from them. This will take on the form of mentorship in a backdoor way.
2. Be tactful and approach your potential mentor in a way that's respectful of his/her time and space. Don't bombard the would-be mentor with tons of emails, texts, and phone calls without their response. Approach him/her with respect and give them enough time and space to reply to you.
3. Find someone that would be likely to help you based on their experiences, background, and current activities. Find

someone that you have something in common with, where you can add value to them on a regular basis so they would be interested in helping you.

4. Many mentors will test your dedication by giving you a small task to see how dedicated you are towards achieving your goal. Give 110% to everything you do. This will show your potential mentor that you value his/her time and will take this opportunity seriously.

Look for Large Acquisitions to Move the Needle

"Only when the tide goes out do you discover who's been swimming naked."

—Warren Buffett

An investor questioned Buffet on what acquisitions Berkshire Hathaway was looking to make. Buffet mentioned several billion dollars being the minimum value of the companies Berkshire would consider acquiring. Buffett said that he could gain 50% returns per year if he had a much smaller amount of money to deploy, but with the scale in amount of money Berkshire is looking to invest currently (as it is quite large), they're looking for large acquisitions to move the needle cash flow-wise and value add-wise.

This concept is wildly important in real estate investing as well. Many naïve investors go after cheap prices and numerous transactions that take much longer to move the needle very much for their overall wealth.

Example (each owns properties at 75% LTV):

Investor A: Buys 20 single-family homes one at a time for $20k each = $400,000 portfolio value

Investor B: Buys 4 single-family homes one at a time for $100k each = $400,000 portfolio value

Investor C: Buys 1 four-plex for $400k = $400,000 portfolio value

Which investor moved the value needle faster? Answer:
Investor C

Systematize and Grow

"Systems make the ordinary extraordinary."
—John Maxwell

Creating a system is the number one thing you need to be shooting for when building your real estate business. There are only so many hours in the day that you can produce, so you will quickly hit your ceiling if you do not leverage others. Smart business people leverage other people's time and other people's money to produce exceptional growth. Watch the movie "The Founder," and you will see that Ray Kroc did this to perfection. Ray Kroc noticed that most hamburger shops are run in a very slow way with no system. He took McDonald's and created a well-oiled machine of a system that cranked out hamburgers and French fries at an incredibly fast rate with quality. It caught on like wildfire and McDonald's has been going gangbusters ever since.

Systematizing your business can be applied to real estate in many different ways. One way is through brokerage. Open your brokerage and hire an executive assistant or admin to leverage their time and to help you gain more traction and do more deals. Bring in agents to help you sell more and manage the agents instead of you trying to make all the sales yourself. Acquire other brokerages and grow your business that way. Work on your business and not in your business. Systematize your business as quickly as possible and you will experience outsized results.

Hearing No

*"It's not hard to make decisions when
you know what your values are."*

—Roy Disney

One thing that one must get used to quickly in real estate investing is the concept of being okay with hearing the word no. Here are a few ways this applies to real estate investing:

- Can I buy your house at 70% of asking price?
- Can I buy your house? I know it isn't listed....
- Would you like to join my brokerage?
- Would you like to invest in a deal I found? I am offering a good return to my equity investors....
- Mom/Dad—I think I want to devote my career to investing in real estate...what do you think?

And the list goes on. One common factor I have noticed amongst very successful investors is their resilience to hearing no. They just don't care. Many started off in some sort of sales role and got very used to hearing the word no, to the point that it became a game to fight through the no. And on the other side of all the nos, is a yes. And when you get the yes, there is value to be had.

Many times the key to getting the yes is to first understand the context of the no. Why is someone saying no? Maybe they need a certain thing from their investment that they don't believe you are offering, but you indeed could offer in order to turn their no into a yes. Press into no to fully understand why before moving on.

Setting and Accomplishing Goals

*"The game has its ups and downs, but you can never
lose focus of your individual goals and you can't
let yourself be beat because of lack of effort."*

—Michael Jordan

I truly believe we are basically limited only by our own perception of what is possible when it comes to smart real estate investing.

My partner and I set a goal to acquire $2 million in cash flow real estate properties this year, with no more than $1.5 million in debt. Our five year goal is to acquire $10 million in cash flow real estate with no more than $7.5 million in debt. At a 3.0% appreciation rate, this $10 million in real estate should be worth roughly $21 million in twenty-five years. After paying back our equity investors, that would leave us with about $10 million per partner.

Crazy, right?

Actually, it's not. Anyone can do it. How, you might ask? Simple. Back into your numbers.

1. How much asset value do you want to have when you are finished? Let's say $10 million per partner x two partners = $20 million

2. How long do you have to make this? Twenty-five years (I chose 25 years because I will be 60 and retirement age)

3. What approximate appreciation rate do you need to meet or exceed this number? 3% (Calculated by the following formula: $10,000,000 \times 1.03^{25}$)

4. In what markets can you reasonably assume a future annual appreciation rate of 3% or better per year?

Find a market that is growing in population, employment, and has shown 3% or greater appreciation per year over the last twenty-five years. Read and do your homework. You will find them.

5. What avenue do you choose to purchase your initial goal amount (here, we'll say $10 million) in real estate?
   a. If you go single-family, you will need fifty houses x $200k per house
   b. If you go multifamily, you will need ten $1 million-dollar complexes
   c. If you go self storage, you will need five $2 million-dollar self storage facilities
6. How will you make traction over time?
   a. Single-family: you should buy ten homes per year, each averaging $200k in value
   b. Multifamily: you should buy two apartment complexes per year, each averaging $1 million
   c. Self storage: you should purchase one self storage facility complex per year, averaging $2 million per facility
7. You don't have that much cash! How will you be able to buy this amount of real estate?

Bring in an investor to front the cash. Incentivize them to their liking and yours.

If you follow this line of logic to create and execute your goals, you could—like me and my partner—look up in five years and find that you have acquired $10 million in cash flow real estate with $7.5 million in debt with future value (in 25 years) of $21 million in real estate on your hands.

Hold or Sell

"Mathematics expresses values that reflect the cosmos, including orderliness, balance, harmony, logic, and abstract beauty."

—Deepak Chopra

I must confess—something inside me gets giddy when I hear investors talk about how they don't sell anything. I feel the excitement of a little kid on Christmas morning. It's so smart. Let's walk through why.

When you flip a house, you have a job.

When you own cash flow real estate, you own an asset.

One could put you out on the street if the deals dry up. One will make you very wealthy.

Now all you flippers hold your horses. I love flipping houses and have done many flips myself. But I do it knowing my profits will be invested in cash flow rental properties that I am keeping long term.

Let's look at a hypothetical situation that many of us experience.

We have purchased a distressed property and fixed it up. It is now in great shape, and our financial picture is as follows:

Cash Invested: $10k
Property Debt: $150k
Property Value: $200k
Monthly Property Market Rent $1,700
Monthly Net Profit: $200
Yearly Net Profit: $2,400
Appreciation Rate Per Year: 3.5%

Principle Pay Down Per Year: $5k (this is flat for simplicity's sake)

Closing Costs Required to Sell: 8% (6% for agent fees + 2% for misc. closing costs)

Sales Price: $200k

The math:

$200k—$16,000 (closings costs) = $184,000–$150,000 = $34,000. We initially invested $10,000, and receive $34,000 back, so we have a net profit of $24,000. Now we must pay short term capital gains tax (estimated at 25%) on our $24k. Taxes = $24k x .25 = $6,000

<u>Flip Profit Net of Taxes: $24k–$6k = $18k</u>

If we hold it as a rental property for 30 years until it is paid off:

Total Value

$2,400 net cash flow profit per year x 30 = $72,000 (let's say we love our tenants and only raise our rents to cover any increase in taxes and insurance)

Property Value = $200k x 3.5% appreciation per year for 30 years = $200k x 1.03^{30} = $561,000

Total Profit: $72,000 + $561,000 = $633,000 - $10,000 initial investment = $623,000

So in these scenarios, our options are $18k profit today or $623,000 profit in 30 years. To get $623k profit in 30 years, your $18k would have to compound at an annual rate of 12.5% per year for the next 30 years. 12.5% may not seem like a big deal when only looking at one year, but compounded over 30 years, it becomes a very big deal.

The wealthy hold on to their properties for the long term to capitalize on this high rate of compounding instead of taking the quick cash influx from the flip and then spending the money or simply having the money sit in their bank account and compound at a rate near zero.

The takeaways:

Long-term investors build wealth.

Flippers have a job.

There is a big difference between the two.

Growth Mind-Set vs Poverty Mind-Set

"Values aren't buses...they're not supposed to get you anywhere. They're supposed to define who you are."

—Jennifer Crusie

To be successful in real estate investing, you must have an abundance mind-set. Those who fail at real estate are on the other side of the fence grazing the grass of the poverty mind-set. Stay out of that pasture.

Let's look at the differences:

Growth Mind-Set
- I can do it regardless of the market cycles
- I can do it regardless of my limited resources
- I can work smarter and harder and achieve my goals
- My failure = learning
- My success = learning
- My failure is my own fault
- I can create a massive goal and achieve it by breaking it down to small achievable goals and conquering them on a daily basis
- I may not have the money, expertise, or time to do a deal, but I can find someone to partner with that can fill those gaps to make the deal possible
- I was just told no—it is only a matter of time until I hear a yes
- Giving creates more opportunity and will always come back

Poverty Mind-Set

- I can't do it because of the market cycle
- I can't do it because I don't have _____ (fill in the blank)
- I am not smart enough and my efforts won't be enough to make me successful
- My failure = my lot in life
- My success = very unlikely
- My failure is someone else's fault
- I shouldn't make a large goal because I am not able to accomplish something like that
- I am stuck.
- I was just told no—I guess this just won't work.

Our minds are a battlefield both on the spiritual level as well as the goal setting level. Make sure your thoughts fall in line with the abundance mind-set instead of the poverty mind-set. It will make all the difference.

Fall in Love with the Process

"There is strange comfort in knowing that no matter what happens today, the sun will rise again tomorrow."

—Aaron Lauritsen, *100 Days Drive: The Great North American Road Trip*

The winningest current college coach in college football is Nick Saban. Coach Saban is known for repeatedly talking about falling in love with the process. Follow the process. Everything is a process. It is no wonder that with predictable regularity he wipes the floor with opponents. Love him or hate him, you have to take your hat off to his dogged determination of breaking everything down to a process and then perfecting that process through repetition.

How do we block? There is a process.
How do we run routes? There is a process.
How do we drop back to pass and check through our receivers? There is a process.
How do we tackle in the open field? There is a process.
How do we celebrate touchdowns? There is a process.

Let's apply this to our real estate business.

How do you find deals? Nail down your process.
How do you fund deals? Nail down your process.
How do you find contractors? Nail down your process.
How do you buy properties outside your local market? Nail down your process.
How do we analyze deals? Nail down your process.

How do you scale? Nail down your processes first, then grow.

It is far better for Nick Saban to lay out the processes and make sure his coaches are enforcing the execution of those processes than it is for Nick to try to coach every player himself. It works the same way in real estate. Iron out your process, get the right people involved in each process, and work *on* the business.

Build Your Reputation

"Reputation is your most important asset. Everything you do, everything you say, is part of the permanent record. Your name reflects your character."

—Sam Zell, *Am I Being Too Subtle*

This is very simple advice, but very important. Doing your first deal is far more important than you making money on your first deal. The reason it is better to do your first deal as opposed to making money, is because getting your first deal behind you is likely the linchpin to take you to baller status as a real estate investor. Remember little Mario running around and then getting a mushroom? This is what happens when you get your first deal behind you. Going forward you can now advertise that you have successfully done a deal and have that knowledge and experience. Deals done lead to street cred. Street cred in this game is more important than anything—even than cash in the bank. Street cred can get you cash in the bank in a phone call or email, and can make deals close. You must build your street cred, and getting your first deal done is the key.

In summary, reputation is more important than money in the real estate game. If you have built a great reputation in the real estate circles, you can literally buy deals with none of your own money simply because people trust you. They trust you to do what you say you will do, and they trust your insight. Guard your reputation at all costs. It is far more important to leave a deal with your reputation intact than it is to leave a deal with profit. If your reputation gets ruined, it may be hard for you to continue doing deals at all.

Passing Can Be a Terrible Decision

"The worst decisions I've ever made were decisions not to take action on good investments."

—Charlie Munger, The Berkshire
Hathaway Shareholder Meeting

Buffett and Munger were asked about the worst decisions they have made throughout their career.

Munger spoke up and said (paraphrased), "The worst decisions I've ever made were decisions not to take action on good investments instead of decisions to take action and the results turning out poorly."

The application to real estate is very straightforward. Many times we have a good deal right in front of us and won't pull the trigger. Our inaction leads to some of our worst decisions whereas our action can lead to both positive and negative results. We won't get the exceptional results without taking action, and this is Munger's point. By taking action we will yield great results over time by learning through trial and error and not giving up. This leads to increased investor IQ and the eventually the results that we all shoot for. Also know this—inaction on a poor opportunity is wise, and can help you avoid some of the biggest mistakes you could make.

Love the Game

"Love is a verb."

—Steven Pressfield, *The War of Art*

Love means action. If you love something, you work after it with reckless abandon. If you love someone, your actions show it. Love isn't a point in time; it is a constant movement towards and unrelenting drive by an energy that can only be called love.

I am a big fan of podcasts, and a big fan of real estate, so naturally one of my favorite podcasts is the *Bigger Pockets* podcast. I listened to this podcast for years, and grew to love the hosts. When I started my own podcast, *The Daily Real Estate Investor*, Brandon Turner (host of the *Bigger Pockets* podcast) was my very first interview. Brandon was gracious enough to let me interview him as a new podcaster, and we kept in touch. Month after month, we would email or text about real estate deals or books we were reading. He was always gracious enough to keep chatting despite being bombarded by everyone and their brother as the *BP* podcast reached 2 million downloads per month.

One *BP* episode, Brandon mentioned starting his own mobile home park investment business. Brandon said "if you are interested in doing analysis for our business, send me a message and we can see if it would be a good fit.

My knee jerk reaction was, "I am interested as I was formally the mobile home park and apartment specialist on my appraisal team at CBRE, but what are the chances they want me? And if they do want me, what are the chances the pay me anything for my time? I guess I shouldn't mess with it."

Then I took a second and thought a little deeper on the subject. "I have a good relationship with Brandon and would absolutely love to work with him long term. Maybe I would make the cut—I have experience and am good with analysis. Even if I worked for free, it would be a great way to establish an even better relationship with someone I respect tremendously and would love to work with. I shouldn't self-select out, but should make them eliminate me instead of preemptively eliminating myself."

I sent Brandon an email expressing my interest in joining their team. Days passed and heard nothing. A couple weeks after my initial message, I received a response from Brandon.

"Interesting. Fill out this application and take this personality profile test and send the results to me at this address," he said. I did everything that was requested. Another week passed, and I received another message. "You passed the first round test, and now we have a second round test. Here is a mobile home park deal we are looking at buying and our complicated Excel model for analyzing the deal. Research and analyze this deal and give us your recommended purchase price and strategy. We need this back in a few days.

I rolled up my sleeves and spent almost an entire day working on this deal. Once I knew I had turned over every stone and done the very best I could, I submitted the final analysis with my recommendation. In a few days I received the following message.

"We had a massive amount of applicants. If you are receiving this message, you made the final cut. You are a rock star! Our offer to you is equity in each deal you help us land. You will do analysis for us, and we will send you leads. If this works for you, reply with yes." I replied yes.

You have to be in the game and grinding to be winning at the game. Don't self-select out. Be bold, embrace the possibility of embarrassment and failure, and you will be shocked what will materialize.

Your Why

*"We must do our work for its own sake, not
for fortune or attention or applause."*

—Steven Pressfield, *The War of Art*

To build your system, you will need a team. To build a team, you will
need properly aligned incentives. To create properly aligned incentives,
you will need to understand what motivates your team. And they will
need to understand what motivates you—your "why."

Your "why" should be clearly defined, and be something that is
deeply motivating to you. I surmise that a noble why is much more
motivating than a vanity metric.

A noble "why" would be, "I want enough passive income to do
work I love full-time and spend more time with my family."

We must do the work for its own sake. This is our art form. This is
our talent and our gift to the world. We don't do this only for fortune
or applause. And if you are doing it for those reasons, take a step
back and seriously analyze why you believe you need the fortune and
applause. Are you trying to seek validation through these channels?
It will undoubtedly leave you empty.

Jim Carrey said, "I think everybody should get rich and famous
and do everything they ever dreamed of so they can see that it's not
the answer."

Do the work for the sake of the work and not the notoriety. Let
your why give you that inner strength to persist, and remember that
when you go out, it all goes to someone else. You can't hang on to it.

Learning Tip:

I asked my CPA about the best way to track my business expenses using a credit card. Here was his response:

"It is always better to get credit cards in the business name for tax purposes. Lots of people don't and just use a personal credit card, but in case of an audit, and really to keep the asset protection in place it's better to get them in the business name. If you comingle personal and business funds, and if someone were to sue you, they could try to get personal assets too instead of just business assets. And again, for asset protection services, you should keep each business separate from each other, so I would get cards in each of the business names."

How to Structure Your First Syndication Deal

*"Most homes valued at over $250,000 have a
library. That should tell you something."*

—Jim Rohn

So you have decided to go big or go home, and want to do your first
syndication deal. How should the syndication be structured? The
answer: it depends.

There are many ways to structure syndication, and the most
important factors to consider are:

1. What is everyone bringing to the table?
2. What does everyone want?

Typically a syndicator will find a deal, then go out and put equity,
debt, and management pieces in place to buy the deal, do value add,
manage the deal, and dispose of the deal (if disposal is the goal). The
syndicator is known as the GP or General Partner (also known as
Sponsor or Syndicator), and is tasked with putting the deal together.
The equity investors are qualified investors and are known as LPs or
Limited Partners. Essentially, the LPs put in cash, and the GPs put
the deal together and make the deal happen. The GPs may put in
some cash as well, typically on the LP side of the equation. The LPs
are passive investors and the GPs are active.

The GPs are owners of the formed partnership and have unlimited
liability in the deal. The GP is responsible for choosing a market, raising
money from passive investors, putting the right team together, and

running point on the syndication start to finish. The GP is generally made up of multiple individuals, although it is possible for only one person to be involved on the GP side. The GP side may include a property manager, or the manager may be an independent third party.

The LPs have limited liability based on the partner's share of the ownership. The LPs are passive investors. LPs contribute equity to the deal in exchange for ownership and are hands off and do not control the strategy of the syndication. The LP side of the deal can be multiple parties or only one.

There are laws around soliciting investment capital for syndications, so check with a real estate attorney before raising money for your deals. Know the difference between an accredited investor and a sophisticated investor, and know the rules around taking money from both.

How is the GP and LP split structured? Everything is negotiable, but there are some general ways many syndications are structured. Most times, total profits are split between the GP and LP, and that split varies based on what each party brings to the table and what they want. This includes experience, equity, time, etc. The split will range from 50/50 to 90/10 Limited Partner to General Partner. The 50/50 split is generally reserved for the seasoned veteran GP while 70/30 split is for the less experienced GP. The LPs may receive a preferred return on their equity investment, and after that preferred return has been met, the remaining profits are generally split based on the agreed split (50/50 or 70/30 as shown above). This preferred return is a return on capital for the LP, and not a return of capital. If the property is sold, the equity investors are paid back the remainder of their equity investment with any accrued interest and then the profit is split based on the deal structure (50/50 or 70/30 as shown above).

Many times there may be an acquisition fee (to the GP), and guaranty fee (to someone acting as a loan guarantor), an asset management fee (to the GP for ongoing oversight and management of the deal, not property management), etc. These fees all vary, but provide an excellent option to the GP for making some money from closing and managing a deal.

At the end of the day, there are many way that a syndication can be structured, so there are no hard and fast rules. The info listed above is subject to the desires of the parties involved. Syndication is a wonderful way for an investor to scale quickly by using other people's money.

Build Your Network

"You can have everything in life you want if you will just help enough other people get what they want."

—Zig Ziglar

There is a principle in real estate that may be even more important that knowing what you are doing. This principle is the concept of building your network. The best real estate investors focus on building their networks and those networks turn into deals.

On an episode of the *Daily Real Estate Investor* podcast, I interviewed Frank DeSalvo who works in self storage syndications. Frank shared a story about spending 40 phone calls networking with the same individual before that owner decided to do a joint venture with Frank's company on the self storage facility that the gentleman owned. Frank's company partnered with the gentlemen and doubled the size of the existing self storage facility, then got the vacant units leased up. Because the two teamed up, massive value was created, and both parties made out like bandits. It took 40 phone calls though, so this didn't happen overnight. Frank spent a lot of time networking with the owner before this deal transpired. Real estate is a relationship business, and networking is perhaps the most important thing you can do to explode your business to exceptional levels.

Learning Tip: A great way to network with other investors is to join your local real estate investor meetups. If there isn't a local meetup, then start one. If you are the one who starts your local real estate investment group, you will be at the center of everything that goes on, which gives you a tremendous opportunity to make great connections, help people accomplish their goals, and make them aware of what your goals are.

My Worst Investment Ever

*"Give me six hours to chop down a tree and I
will spend the first four sharpening the ax."*

—Abraham Lincoln

I was interviewed by Andrew Stotz on his podcast titled, *My Worst
Investment Ever*. I also published the episode on my podcast, *The Daily
Real Estate Investor*. On the episode I shared the hilarious and painful
story of flip that didn't work out so well.

My partner and I ended up losing $30,000 on the flip, but even
worse, our investment business ground to a halt. We put all deal
hunting and acquisitions on hold as we dealt with this fire spitting
dragon of a property. The street name was Wildflower, but the only
thing true about that name was the Wild portion. This was no flower.
This Wild beast tortured us for 6 months and then made its depar-
ture through sale leaving us with $30k less than we started with and
exhausted spirits.

Things that went wrong:

- Failure to properly estimate repair costs
- Declined to do a property inspection
- Priced the property too high when listing
- Trusted inaccurate listing info when buying (didn't
  verify everything)
- Took on a project too far from the city center which equaled
  fewer buyers
- Didn't pay proper attention to the average days on the market
  for sales in the subject's

- Didn't properly estimate holding costs (we planned to hold it for 3 months and ended up owning it a total of 9 months)
- Armadillo investigation
- Ground hornet yard infestation
- Four rounds of inspections due to selling the property to a VA buyer
- Septic issues
- Foundation issues
- Missed rotten wood around windows

Need I say more? When we sold this property, we celebrated. We celebrated more than we did when we sold flips making $20k or $30k. We were so glad to have this clog out of our system finally!

The takeaway here is a failure in proper planning, plain and simple. We rushed through our analysis and were so happy to be doing a deal, that we missed the flashing red lights warning us to tread very carefully. It is far better to over plan and not do the deal than plan too little and buy a bad deal and it stall your entire investing system.

Learning Tip: When running numbers on a flip, build in a contingency factor or a cushion. Some successful flippers factor in a 20% contingency factor. This gives you a 20% mulligan before you start eroding profit. It is the tendency of investors to underestimate rehab costs and overestimate sales price. Use this contingency factor to protect yourself from your own buyer bias. It will save you doing some deals you should have passed on. And if things go well, you will make more money than you had anticipated.

Communication Breakdown

*"To effectively communicate, we must realize that we are
all different in the way we perceive the world and use this
understanding as a guide to our communication with others."*

—Tony Robbins

If there is one thing that will destroy a deal being done, it is poor
communication. Many times a deal could be held together by a level-
headed phone call to get on the same page with another party. Someone
doesn't like the way a text reads or a few lines in an email, and a case
is built in their head against the other party. Sometimes a mountain is
created from a molehill, and sometimes the other party is truly being
difficult. Regardless—I have found that 99% of these issues can be
solved by picking up the phone and connecting with the other party
for a brief chat with a respectful tone and ability for empathy. Seek
first to understand, and then to be understood. Allow the other party
to be wrong with dignity and not embarrassment, and show humility.
If communication breaks down, your deal will fall apart. And we get
no badge of honor for the deals that get away.

When to Fire

"Dealing with employee issues can be difficult.
Not dealing with them can be worse."

—Paul Foster

Firing someone is never fun, but there isn't a more necessary thing in creating a successful real estate venture. I was given the advice that when you have a bad hire, fire them as quickly as you have recognized that fact. I just fired a property manager, and we just hired another. It has already made a massively positive impact. The first property manager had multiple people interested in renting our property, but wasn't returning inquiries in a timely fashion. The new hire already has the property up and we are about to sign a lease on it. The real difference comes in that we have a good deal of properties that will be under new management with this new manager, and so if our properties are optimized even 10%, it makes a big impact on the bottom line. We didn't have a contract with our old property manager for this very reason, and I am glad I didn't.

For example, let's say you have 10 properties renting for on average for $1,500 per month. It normally takes 30 days to find a new tenant once the property is vacant and marketed for lease, but your less than energetic property manager isn't proactive and therefore it takes you 60 days to get your property leased. 1 month vacancy x 10 properties x $1,500 per month = $15,000. Your mediocre property manager is costing you lost income amounting to $15,000 in this example! It is far better to pay a slightly higher management fee and get a rock star who will keep your properties optimized than to try to cut corners with a cheap management fee and get someone who doesn't give your portfolio the attention it deserves.

The Power of a Mentor

"A mentor is someone who sees more talent and ability within you, than you see in yourself, and helps bring it out of you."

—Bob Proctor

Email exchange with my mentor who had a bigger impact on my investing game than I could have imagined:

Mentor,

Are you open to having me as a coaching client? I plan to pursue building my multifamily business hardcore now, and I would like to have someone I compensate in some form or fashion to bounce questions off of on a weekly basis and have a strategy/ progress call with every couple of weeks.

I would love to have you as my coach, and truly believe I can make it worth your time as I begin to close these deals. I want to go big with this so I can help as many people as possible, so I want to set myself up for success. Are you open to that, and if so, how could we do it to make you happy?

Josiah

Thanks Josiah!

It was really great to spend some time with you this past weekend. I'm excited to see what you can do! I don't think I'd be comfortable charging you for coaching. I've never done that and there are a lot of reasons why, but we can save that conversation for another day. That said, I'm glad to continue to serve as your mentor in some capacity with the goal of potentially someday having a partner relationship. Why don't we plan to have bi-weekly calls with the idea that when you get a deal we can figure out an arrangement that makes sense where I can partake in the upside? How does that sound?

Mentor

Mentor,
Best email I have received all year! Thank you so much! You don't know how much this means to me.

Josiah

My mentor had a thriving real estate portfolio and business, but took a chance and invested in me, and it made all the difference in my life. I exhibited work ethic, drive, and a willingness to learn. To get and keep a great mentor, you must do the same. Be careful though—there are many posing as mentors that will take a large sum of money in exchange for little value. Be sure to properly vet your potential mentor with those who have experience with that mentor and can vouch for its value. I spent a good bit of time getting to know my mentor before approaching him on the mentorship/coaching idea, and I truly believe that is why he agreed. If you approach someone that doesn't know you and is a busy person, they are likely to decline unless you are paying them (and well in most situations). Be very cautious while pursuing a mentor/coach—you stand to lose your time and money if you choose poorly.

Scale Both Vertically
and Horizontally

"Growth is never by mere chance; it is the result of forces working together."

—James Cash Penney

If your goal is to scale your real estate portfolio, it is very important to attack the scaling process with a plan. Too many investors try to scale by doing the following:

Year	Purchase	Portfolio
Year 1	1 House	1 Door
Year 2	1 House	2 Doors
Year 3	1 House	3 Doors

This is an example of scaling vertically, but not horizontally. Vertical scaling is occurring by adding one house per year to the portfolio. This is the hardest and least efficient way to scale. The above example will work, but at a much slower pace.

Instead, a much more efficient way to scale would be scaling both vertically (adding numbers) and horizontally (adding larger and larger deal size) as follows:

Year	Purchase	Portfolio
Year 1	1 House	1 Door
Year 2	20 Unit Apartment Complex	21 Doors
Year 3	100 Unit Apartment Complex	121 Doors

By scaling both vertically and horizontally, massive wealth will be created in a much more efficient manner and in much less time. The best investors I have met mastered this concept and never looked back.

The Lifecycle of a Rehab Rental

*"The perfect orchestration of the symphony of life is one
of the Creator's greatest and most beautiful miracles."*

—Suzy Kassem

There is a predictable flow and cycle that is observed when one purchases a distressed property, does value add rehab, and leases the property.

Typical cycle:

1. Purchase—in this phase, the property is typically vacant and distressed. The property is not stabilized and unable to produce income in its current state.

2. Rehab—the new owner has purchased the vacant unstabilized property and begins rehabbing the property. Although the property is moving towards a stabilized state, if one stops in the middle of the renovation, a discounted price will be required to sell the property and it will be difficult to rent.

3. Available For Rent—property has now been renovated and is rent ready. The property is able to make money, but needs a tenant to drive that income stream. Tenants are screened and an application is approved.

4. Rented— the new tenant moves in and discovers a number of issues in their new place.

5. Tenant Requests— tenant requests move-in repairs. Without fail, nearly every rental I have owned has a tenant request a list of repairs just after moving in. Sometimes the list is long

and sometimes the list is short. Don't be discouraged—this phase is to be expected and will pass.

6. Happy Tenant—repairs have been made and the tenant settles in to their new rental. The property has now reached peak stabilization and peak cash flow as it is fully rented and provides cash flow.

This life-cycle is to be expected and one must remember not to be discouraged at any step along this process as, with persistence, it will lead to a stabilized cash flow rental.

The Power of Written Goals

"People with clear, written goals, accomplish
far more in a shorter period of time than people
without them could ever imagine."

—Brian Tracy

Written goals are so important. Write your goals down and take massive action, and see what happens. My business partner and I put the following 12-month goal in writing:

Goal for 2019–Jan 1, 2019

Purchase 10 rental properties by Dec 31, 2019
Location: B-class neighborhoods
Strategy: BRRRR Strategy (BRRRR = Buy, Rehab, Rent, Refinance, and Repeat).
Equity: 25% or greater
Value Per Property: $200k average
Monthly Net Profit Per Door (Avg): $200

Goal Update—Nov. 30, 2019

Completed Purchase of 15 properties
Location: B-Class Neighborhoods
Strategy: BRRRR Strategy
Value: $3,000,000
Equity: $900,000
Equity: 30%
Value Per Property: $200,000
Monthly Net Profit Per Door (Avg): $208.50

How to Accomplish a Goal

"Set your goals high, and don't stop till you get there."

—Bo Jackson

Regarding the former page—I was asked: how did you build a $3 million portfolio in 15 cash flow rentals using the BRRRR Strategy so quickly?

1. Worked my butt off
2. Ran my own business allowing me flexibility of time to pursue deals each day
3. Built relationships with wholesalers to provide leads
4. Had clearly identified buying criteria
5. Developed relationships with private/hard money lenders
6. Had local market knowledge
7. Had equity and raised more equity
8. Had boots on the ground to run projects
9. Vetted contractors and had capable contractor teams
10. Looked at 20 properties to offer on 1
11. Persisted through renovation issues
12. Managed capital during simultaneous renos and refis
13. Had a great management company
14. Didn't quit
15. Got very quiet in my own head. Tuned out negativity and focused.

Make no mistake—it didn't happen overnight, and it was a daily struggle. Real estate is a problem-solving business, and the problems to be solved don't stop coming. But it is a beautiful thing to look at a property that you took from vacant and falling apart to occupied and beautiful, and it is satisfying to know you created an outsized return on investment by going your own way.

The Flip Formula

"Every day is a bank account, and time is our currency.
No one is rich, no one is poor, we've got 24 hours each."

—Christopher Rice

When flipping a house, it is important to run the right numbers to make sure you will make a satisfactory return on the deal. Here is how most house flippers calculate their buy price.

> 70% Rule in House Flipping:
> ARV (After Repair Value): $200k
> ARV of $200k X 70% = $140k
> $140k—Repairs of $20,000
> = Purchase Price of $120,000 or less
> Let's work these numbers going the other directions:
> ARV: $200k
> Purchase Price: $120k
> Repairs: $20k
> Holding Costs: $10k
> Closing Costs on Initial Purchase: $5k
> Sales Price: $200K
> Closing Costs on Flip Sale at 8% of sales price: $16,000
> Net Profit = $200k–$20k–$10k–$5k–$16k–$120k = $29k

Assuming these respective numbers are accurate, a flipper would walk away with approximately $29k profit on this deal. Always over-estimate repairs and holding costs and underestimate potential after repair sales price. This will help you avoid buying deals where margins are too thin and getting yourself into trouble.

The 1% Rule

"What we fear doing most is usually what we most need to do."
—Tim Ferriss, The 4 Hour Workweek

Many investors use the 1% rule as a quick way to determine if a property has positive cash flow potential net of operating expenses and debt service. If it does not meet or exceed the 1% rule, it may indicate potentially dangerous cash flow issues.

1% Rule formula: Gross Monthly Rent/Total Property Cost.

Example:
Gross Monthly Rent: $1,500
Total Property Cost: $125,000
1% Test: $1,500/$125,000 = 1.2%

In the example above, this property has a 1.2% rent ratio, indicating that it may produce positive cash flow. The higher the rent ratio, the better the cash flow margin. Some investors look for a rent ratio of 2% or more. Typically, a property's quality of location has an inverse correlation as the rent ratio goes up or down. An example of this inverse correlation can be seen as follows:

A Class Rental: 0.8% rent ratio
B Class Rental: 1.2% rent ratio
C Class Rental: 2.0% rent ratio

Trusting Wholesalers

"I am more afraid of an army of one hundred sheep led by
a lion than an army of one hundred lions led by a sheep."

—Charles Maurice

Working with wholesalers on building my single-family portfolio was a game changer for me. Wholesalers get a bad rap sometimes, but they certainly serve a purpose in the real estate investing food chain. I believe they can get a bad rap from time to time because some wholesalers operate beyond the boundaries of ethical activity—but that applies to any real estate professional. If someone is acting unethically—they should receive a bad rap.

Here is how to find a great wholesaler:

- Network with as many wholesalers as possible
- Join as many wholesaler lists as possible
- When a wholesaler tells you one thing and does another, move their emails to your spam folder and don't work with them again
- When a wholesaler keeps their word and closes a deal, prioritize that wholesaler going forward

The 80/20 rule certainly applies to wholesalers. 80% are not worth working with and 20% are, with the 20% bringing in over 80% of the deals you will close. Find a couple good wholesalers and the deals will flow. Keep your word and they will love working with you. It seems simple, but 1 in every 2 people in real estate don't keep their word.

Here is how we spot a good wholesale deal:

- For buy and holds: we can be all in for 75% loan-to-value or less. This includes purchase price (with wholesaler assignment fee), closing costs, holding costs, repair costs, and refinance costs.
- For flips: ARV (after-repair-value) x 70%–repairs = Purchase Price. If we can get it for equal to or less than our purchase price figure in this formula, we are interested.
- The property is located in our target acquisition area
- We are comfortable with the scope of repair work
- We have a contractor team that services the area we are buying in
- We have good comparable sales and rents that clearly comp our value. Always pull your own comps and never rely on the value the wholesaler advertises or their repair estimate.

When you find a good deal and are well positioned to take it down, don't be afraid to do so. Networking is the key to finding good wholesalers, and filtering out the good from the bad is also a must. If you put in the work, it will pay off big time by the deals you start seeing.

Fall in Love with a Property Type and Go for It

To make an embarrassing admission, I like video games. That's what got me into software engineering when I was a kid. I wanted to make money so I could buy a better computer to play better video games—nothing like saving the world.

—Elon Musk

"How do I know which areas to target for my apartment search?"—me

"You know which areas in your town you would own and which areas you would avoid right?"—mentor

"Oh yes."—me

"Then target those areas you know."—mentor

It seems rather complicated when you transition from single-family investing into multifamily, but it really isn't. Here is how to find and close your first apartment deal:

- Start in your local market and target areas you know and would like to own in
- Network with each and every property owner of those respective apartment buildings in your target area
- Be persistent—stay in touch with these owners once or twice a month until deals start materializing.
- Network with each and every broker in your target area. Let them know exactly what you are looking for. They will ask questions of your experience and resources.
- Fill in your knowledge and experience gaps with an investing veteran. If you have never closed a deal, find a bigger player

in the multifamily space and incentivize them to provide credibility to your deal as well as advice. You can incentivize a number of ways, one of which is giving them equity in your deal for their time, credibility, and expertise.

- Have the proper amount of resources to close the deal, whether it be yours, or limited partner investors. There are laws around raising money, so make sure to consult with an attorney that specializes in real estate syndication before making any naïve moves.

- Go walk deals and run numbers on deals as much as possible. You will become more comfortable with the numbers and understand what a good deal is. It will likely not happen on your first try, but like anything else, it is a numbers game. If you get 1 in 20 houses you consider in single-family, why would it be any different with multifamily?

- Have a licensed inspector perform an inspection on a deal you are serious about buying. Always and without fail have this done.

- Have proper financing lined up and approved.

- When you find one that meets your acquisition criteria, checks out inspection wise, the numbers work, and your investing veteran gives it the green light, pull the trigger!

Grit or Fail

"Don't ask what's the least you can do. Ask
what's the most you can bear."

—Tom Bilyeu

Real estate investing is about grit. If you don't have grit, you are going to get smoked. You're going to get run over, stolen from, cheated, swindled, and lied to. People are going to try to take your money, they're going to take your time, and they're going to take your emotions. You can't let that bother you.

I'm going to shoot you straight—this is one of the most difficult things I've ever done. But one of the best things I've ever done. If you can persevere, you can do anything with this, I truly mean that. The only thing holding you back is the fear of failure. If you lack capital you can raise it, if you lack knowledge you can gain it, and if you lack hustle you can find a boots-on-the-ground partner. There is no gap you can't backfill, no goal you can't achieve, and no reason you can't set out on this journey. The only thing holding you back is you. Don't say you have goals and then not take action; taking action is the key to reaching your goals and changing your financial future.

A Bird in the Hand Is Worth 20 in the Bush

"What price are you willing to pay for greatness?"

—Tom Bilyeu

In all seriousness I probably look at 20 deals a day, and make an offer on only one or two of those. I've had a few days recently where I've gotten two deals in two days, and there's some weeks where I don't get any deals, over the last 12 months we've landed 15 deals. I would say on average I'm looking at 40 to 60 deals for every deal that we end up getting. In real estate, a bird in the hand (or a property owned) is easily worth 20 in the bush. The difference in real estate between potential purchase and property owned is massive. Don't mistake potential for reality. You must try each potential deal against your own standards and hurdles to ensure that it is a good deal for you. When it meets your criteria stick to your guns and negotiate a price that works for you. Don't falter.

Say When

In one of my very favorite movies, *Tombstone*, Doc Holliday meets Johnny Ringo in an open field to settle a dual.

Doc Holliday looks Johnny Ringo in the face and says, "Say when."

Johnny Ringo, incensed at Doc Holliday's irreverence, pulls his gun and gets blazed by Holliday. In real estate, many times you'll be at a standstill in an open field on a deal with the other party staring you in the eyes saying, "Say when."

Don't lose your cool. Don't get smoked. The party who gets emotional, loses their cool, and makes a rash decision is undoubtedly the party that ends up screwed. Keep your cool in the face of danger, adversity, and your deals—and don't waver. Be Doc Holliday—don't be Johnny Ringo.

The Weight Loss and Buying Properties Plan

"All the opportunity in the world means nothing
if you don't actually pull the trigger."

—Sam Zell, *Am I Being too Subtle?*

Believe it or not, weight loss and physical fitness go hand in hand with building a real estate portfolio. Time and time again, I talk to real estate investors who are making massive traction in their real estate businesses and are at the same time losing weight and become more fit. Take Brandon Turner for example. Over the last year, he purchased a mobile home park, and while hanging out with him in Hawaii, he shared that he has over the last 6 months or so lost about 40 lbs! Incredible, right? We see this same phenomenon with the folks that do the Dave Ramsey plan.

Countless individuals that call in to the Dave Ramsey show to scream "I'm debt free!" also share their stories of significant weight loss as well. Why is this?

It is because the muscle you need to build your real estate portfolio is the same muscle that you also need to lose weight. The muscle is willpower/grit/determination. You come up with a plan, you execute on that plan, and you don't give up until you reach your goal. Period. No other way. Want to lose weight and buy real estate?

Real Estate Investing Can = Fat Loss

Tim Ferris references his Slow Carb diet plan in the *Four Hour Body* and it works like a charm. His plan allows you to eat as much of the following as you like: lean protein (think grilled chicken, grass fed beef, turkey, etc.), beans/legumes, veggies, and good fats (think avocado). Here are the rules for his plan for losing 20 lbs. of fat in 30 days:

- Avoid white carbohydrates (or anything that can be white)
- Eat the same few meals over and over again
- Don't drink calories
- Don't eat fruit
- Take one day off per week and go nuts

Buying a deal works the same way as fat loss. You can make massive traction if you create a system of rules and guidelines to take down a deal. Let's say you want to buy 3 single-family properties in the next 90 days:

- Locate target market
- Identify optimal price point and rent ratio for target area
- Secure financing (hard money, equity, debt through banks, etc.)
- Create a system for making 5 offers per day for the next 90 days by locating local real estate agents that can birddog properties for you and make offers
- If performing value add, properly vet contractor teams and have them ready to roll once you close your deals
- Upon closing, have renovation scheduled agreed upon with contractor in writing with payment hurdles based on work accomplished
- Locate property management company to get properties listed for rent as soon as renovations are complete

If you do the above, I would bet 9 out of 10 times you have 3 properties under contract before your first 30 days have passed. Let's say you live in a very tight market and none of your offers are being accepted. You will need to get more creative in making your deal. Does the property have a space that could be converted into a fourth bedroom? Does the property have two garages (one that could be converted to more heated and cooled square footage - check local permitting rules on this)? Maybe you need to source these deals from wholesalers to make your numbers work, or maybe you can drive neighborhoods and locate off-market properties that have an owner that is in a bind to sell. There are a thousand ways to buy deals, but one way not to. If you don't take action and train the willpower muscle, you won't make progress.

The 90 Challenge: I challenge you to couple the Tim Ferris Slow Carb Diet along with a 90-day property goal. See what magic you can create when you start getting healthier while making massive progress on your real estate goals.

Send me an email at josiahsmelser@gmail.com with your success stories, and I will try to collect and share them. Here's to your success!!

Conclusion

In conclusion, I hope these thoughts have helped you on your investing journey. We investors are brothers and sisters, so know that I am in your corner. Don't give up and you will make it. 95% of your success hinges on your mindset. The other 5% is formulas that can be found in textbooks and on the web. Get your mind right and you got this in the bag.

Please reach out to me and let me know your story, and maybe you can share your investing journey one day on my podcast. If you are interested in my help with your real estate goals or projects, I offer coaching and consulting. Email me and I will be happy to help you on your way. My contact info is below.

Podcast: The Daily Real Estate Investor
Instagram: @dailyrealestateinvestor
Email: josiahsmelser@gmail.com
Website: www.dailyrealestateinvestor.com